Jennifer Berman & Carole Lazarus

GLORAFILIA
the MINIATURE
NEEDLEPOINT
COLLECTION

*Over 16 Exquisitely Small
and Easy-to-Make Projects*

CROWN PUBLISHERS, INC.
New York

Published by Crown Publishers, Inc., 201 East 50th Street, New York,
New York 10022. Member of the Crown Publishing Group.

Random House, Inc., New York, Toronto, London, Sydney, Auckland

Originally published in Great Britain in 1994 by Ebury Press.
Crown is a trademark of Crown Publishers, Inc.

Manufactured in Italy

Design by Polly Dawes
Photographs by Tim Imrie

Library of Congress Cataloging-in-Publication Data is available.

ISBN: 0-517-79986-3

10 9 8 7 6 5 4 3 2 1

First American Edition

CONTENTS

INTRODUCTION ℰ

Who said that more than one of anything is a collection?

We have found that friends who 'collect' are the best people to choose or make presents for: anything related to their collection will be greeted rapturously. The needlepoint projects in this book cover some of the most popular 'collectables', with an emphasis on ease and speed of stitching. They would make excellent gifts for committed collectors, tentative collectors, just hovering-on-the-edge collectors, or not collectors at all!

After many years of producing needlepoint on a more ambitious scale, we have only lately began to enjoy really small needlepoint projects: pieces to be worked in a few hours, that can easily be carried around for travelling. Working small pieces has a charm of its own: the end always in sight!

Carole writes:

Most of us are collectors in one way or another – a quick survey at Glorafilia revealed collectors of antique teapots, gardening tools, perfume bottles, soup ladles, theatre programs, prayer beads and a hotly denying compulsive collector of recipes. Cathy, who worked with us on this book, insisted smugly she didn't collect anything. 'What about hats?' we asked. 'Oh, yes, hats.' 'And the badges, how many badges?' 'Mmm, badges, maybe a hundred.'

The reasons for collecting are fascinating. Perhaps the idea is encouraged in childhood by grouping bricks and putting objects into 'families'. We start with stamp and scrap albums, pencils, records, books . . . Some collections grow modestly, some are obsessive (think of Imelda's

shoes) or bizarre (the Bhagwan's Rolls Royces), practical (husbands) or obscure (ebony quill cutters). Or just overwhelming, like the collection to end them all: the John Soane Museum in London. It would be interesting to know what he collected as a child! Is it the basic desire to acquire, to squirrel away privately or flamboyantly, an exaggerated nesting instinct? Is it the scent of the challenge and the ultimate prize? A childhood deprivation? Or is it just that it's fun?

The sixteen collections that inspired this book are sometimes eccentric, often stunning, always interesting. It was truly a privilege to meet their creators, all of whom are passionate about what they collect, and it altered our thinking about discreet understatement. How much better just to pile it on – excess is great!

Jennifer has a perfect attitude to collecting: enthusiastic enough to have palpitations over a rare plate, but cool enough to stay this side of obsessive. Her dresser of Copeland Spode, shown here, is stunning to look at, and also very interesting because of the sheer variety of the pieces. She has walls and shelves and ledges hung with blue and white jugs and alcoves crammed with Arthur Wood's peachy 1930s' china. For someone unable to rise in the morn, she throws herself out of bed easily enough at the prospect of London's Bermondsey antique market at dawn, or an obscure antique fair in the country. She is in her element buying antique needlework and accessories for the shop, and has a wonderful eye, often knowing exactly who will want a particular piece: collecting by proxy.

My own collecting sneaked up on me. I always

believed I travelled light, all I needed was a futon rolled under my arm, the indispensable jacket, a few slim volumes. When I moved house, two pantechnicons and seventy tea chests proved me a liar. What I had not taken into account was: the kitchen equipment — essentials like chestnut roasters, ancient egg racks, the chains and yoke from two oxen; books — how can you have too many books?; chairs — more chairs than we could ever need: carved, campaign, wicker, gothic, Victorian (you never know when you'll be short of a chair); then the stonework — carvings, heads, busts, plinths, pillars. I knew about the things I formally collected: tiny coffee cups, shells and crystals, Japanese lacquer, primitive little figures, and unpacked and arranged them in their new positions, much the way Linus arranges his security blanket. All the other stuff was a surprise. Wonder how that accumulated, I said, to anyone who was still talking to me.

Jennifer writes:
Barbra Streisand recently sold a collection of Art Nouveau and Art Deco that she had amassed since the age of fifteen — apparently she had loved buying hand-made pieces costing only a few dollars that no-one else had, and later moved into more seriously priced stuff, but the thrill was always the bargain. Perhaps it became harder to find a bargain, or perhaps once she was able to buy at any price, the joy of collecting went. Elton John also collected Art Nouveau and Art Deco, and similarly rid himself of his collection. Since collecting is sometimes associated with a need to create an identity, perhaps neither of them any longer needed the extra baggage associated with being a dedicated collector. It's interesting that they both collected antiques associated with the glamorous era of the entertainment world and began collecting before they were really successful.

What turns ordinary people into passionate collectors? Is it the acquisitive side of nature — does it make us feel secure to have lots of things around us; do we have the desire to own more of

one item than anyone else; is it greed, an addiction, an illness (bitten by the bug), a madness (bibliomania means extreme pre-occupation with collecting books) – or is it simply a hobby? Is it a status symbol or a dinner-table topic? Well, probably all these things.

What category do Carole and I fall into? We are both interested in antiques, we both love beautiful things and can become ecstatic over a bargain. We both kept scrapbooks when we were young: I collected stamps, Carole collected cheese labels. We are definitely acquisitive but not obsessive. We are not connoisseurs on what we collect, nor do we want to own more than anyone else. Perhaps it's a way of indulging ourselves without being too obvious!

Carole began collecting before she had her own home. In the mid-1960s she used to frequent antique shops and, to her parents' horror, bring home large pieces of furniture which she would cram into her bedroom. I couldn't quite understand this desire of hers and thought it eccentric, because I was busy at that time collecting shoes with matching handbags and as many Biba dresses as I could afford. How wrong I was. Carole now has a wonderful collection of antiques bought for a small amount of money,

while my clothes collection has long since gone.

I collect George III Copeland Spode china and Arthur Wood 1930s' china, blue and white jugs, Victorian watercolors, crystal candlesticks and wine glasses. All the glasses are individual and I found several in dingy backstreet shops while working on our Venice book. There seems to be a law with collecting that the most delicate pieces have to be carried the furthest!

What effect does this collecting have on our children? My 12-year-old daughter is a born collector. Since babyhood she has had a room full of teddies and needlepoint animals, dolls from overseas and a Victorian miniature hat collection. She has now added her own identity and is gradually removing my original choice. She collects horse memorabilia and horse rosettes, and spends hours cataloging and sticking horse pictures into scrapbooks. A psychologist might say she is insecure, but I know she is going to be a collector de force!

Carole's daughters gather round themselves as many Indian and Afghan artefacts, textiles and native silver as they can. My son, on the other hand, has the opposite reaction and likes everything minimalistic. The only things he collects are dirty washing and parking tickets!

TEDDY BEARS

Collecting teddy bears has a word of its own: arctophily, formed from the Greek words *arktos* and *philos*, bear and love. When the actor Peter Bull discovered he was not alone in his nostalgia for a lost childhood bear, and wrote his *Teddy Bear Book*, he became the catalyst for generations of bear lovers worldwide, and the arctophily deluge began. As well as covering the history of the teddy bear, this book discussed the great effect a bear can have on his owner's life.

Collectors should buy with their heads as well as their hearts, however much the bear in question looks in need of a home. A bear's provenance is not always easy to identify – in many cases the teddy may be a child's first treasured possession, which means it may have been loved beyond recognition. An ear has perhaps been replaced, the snout repaired, the paws patched, all helping to disguise its origins. Some bears wear tags, or buttons on the ear or under the arm, or labels woven onto the foot, and experience will help the arctophile identify a bear by its elongated nose, or humped back, or distinctive growl, even if it no longer has its 'seal'.

What is the magic of a teddy bear? Is it an uncritical friend, a confidante, a substitute sibling to absorb tears and share memories? We endow them with the characteristics we look for in those closest to us. There was Rupert, and Winnie-the-Pooh (the best bear ever), Brideshead's wonderful Aloysius and, of course, 'Teddy' Roosevelt's famous mascot.

Following President Roosevelt's refusal to shoot a bear on a hunt, the image of bears became linked with him and mass production of the first jointed plush bears began . . . the 'Teddy'. At the same time in Germany, Margarete Steiff had her first real success with her hitherto ignored bears – and at the Leipzig Fair in 1903 received an order for 3,000 bears from a New York store. The bear boom began.

These Steiff bears, recognizable by a trademark button in one ear, have marvellous expressions and character. With embroidered noses and a wistful tilt of the head, they would challenge even the least childlike among us. The Steiff bear which modelled for our needlepoint was one of the most expensive bears ever – he was sold in 1989 for £55,000/US$86,350, and now resides happily in California.

Bears are often preferable to humans. Bears are unlikely to complain that the Napoleon brandy has been finished, or to smoke your last cigarette. Bears don't need orthodontic treatment. As age takes it toll, a bear can be transformed with new stuffing to its thighs, an aspect many of us envy. If a bear has moths or fleas, you can put it in the freezer for two days – not really recommended for humans.

Some arctophiles collect for love, others for indulgence: another bear and another, older, rarer. For collectors, there is always the promise of another attic being cleared and the possibility of an undiscovered bear finding its way into an antique shop or market stall. And ask any bear collector to remember that first teddy and you will see a smile of nostalgia and an offer to show it to you, because they still have it, there on that back shelf.

Approximate time needed: 32 hours
Finished size of design: 23 x 17 cm (8¾ x 6½ in)
Yarns

Key	Anchor Stranded Cotton		Skeins
A	403	Black	1
	Anchor Tapisserie Wool		
B	9402	Oatmeal	2
C	9384	Honey	2
D	9426	Cinnamon	3
E	9428	Brown	2
F	8236	Orange	1
G	8242	Rust	2
H	8792	Blue	2
I	9678	Pale mauve	1
J	8510	Mauve	1
K	8880	Pale green	1
L	9028	Bottle green	2

Canvas

14-gauge white interlock
Size: 33 x 27 cm (12¾ x 10½ in)

Other materials

Tapestry needle, size 20
Ruler or tape measure
Masking tape for binding the canvas
Sharp scissors for cutting the canvas
Embroidery scissors
Sharp HB pencil or fine permanent marker
Eraser

Following the chart

Cut the canvas to size and bind the edges with masking tape. The design does not have to be marked out on the canvas; just follow the color chart opposite. Remember that the squares represent the canvas intersections, not the holes. Each square represents one tent stitch.

The chart is divided into units of 10 squares by 10 squares to make it easier to follow. Before beginning to stitch, it may be helpful to mark your canvas in similar units of 10 squares by 10 squares with an HB pencil or permanent marker in a suitable color. Also, we suggest marking the top of the canvas so that if you turn the canvas while stitching you still know where the top is.

The colors on the chart are shown stronger than the actual yarn colors to make them easier to see. The corresponding yarns are given in the color key.

Stitches used

TENT stitch (1), STEM stitch (2) (optional). For the stitch instructions, see page 90.

Stitching the design

Use the whole thread of tapisserie wool and the whole thread (six strands) of stranded cotton throughout. Begin with TENT stitch (1) in any area you wish. It might be easiest to start at the top right hand corner of the canvas 4–5 cm (1½–2 in) in from the corner of the canvas, working horizontally from one block of color to another. We have used STEM stitch (2) to outline the bears' eyes, noses and mouths, but this is optional. If you decide to use STEM stitch, this should be done after the TENT stitch areas are complete. Refer to the photograph of the finished picture for the position of the STEM stitch.

Making up instructions

Many needlepointers feel experienced enough to stretch and make up their needlepoint designs, but we always feel that a picture should be framed by a professional experienced in stretching and framing needlepoint.

Key

A B C D E F G H I J K L

LACE BOBBINS &

The lace-maker's lot is legendary: starting as young as eight, roomfuls of girls worked by a single tallow candle, and thousands became blind before they were thirty. Machines took over the lace industry in the second half of the nineteenth century, and old lace is now collected and cherished. However, it is one of the lacemaker's tools, the bobbin, that we find most appealing.

Pillow lace has each thread wound onto a bobbin, some patterns needing 200 bobbins or more. Bobbins were made out of sheep or pig bones, or whatever could be found, by simple, often illiterate people for their mothers and sweethearts – the women whom Shakespeare calls in *Twelfth Night* 'the free maids that weave their thread with bones'.

Many bobbins were inscribed with religious tracts, dates of weddings, births, deaths. Frequently messages were romantic: 'Nothing but death shall part us', 'When this you see remember me'. Each happening, good and bad, would be seen on the lacemaker's pillow, representing the story of her life. It was said that when her husband died, the entire pillow went into mourning, with black beads on the bobbins.

Bobbins have different characters: European bobbins are bulbous, English bobbins are slender with weight added by beads or spangles. The Belgians with their austere wooden bobbins say the English need spangles to liven up their otherwise boring lace! Instead of beads, sometimes a lacemaker would thread her own mementos: army buttons, coins, boot buttons, anything as long as it had a hole in it.

The style variations are charming: the Jack-in-the-Box, the Mother'n'Babe (which pulls apart to show a baby inside), Church Windows, carvings within carvings, some inlaid with pewter, some bitted (inset with different woods). One much copied bobbin is called a Kitty Fisher – remember 'Lucy Locket lost her pocket, Kitty Fisher found it'? Kitty was an actress greatly favored by the Prince Regent, while poor Lucy was not. The bobbin has distinctive blue and red spangles representing Kitty's eyes and lips.

People begin collecting bobbins for different reasons – perhaps the best is that they are so beautiful, tactile and glittery that we could all be swooping magpies wanting the pretty things. Doreen Turner, whose bobbins we show here, began collecting when she was captivated by a box of fifty bobbins in an antique shop and thus took up lace-making, instead of the other way round. When she plans a piece of lace, part of the anticipation is imagining how the bobbins will look on the pillow, knowing how certain bobbins will handle, favoring some over others. The creation of the lace is as important as the end result. In her home, one keeps coming across work-in-progress, pillows with exquisite morsels of lace from which hang dozens of shimmering little bobbins.

She feels every bobbin has a history. It was handled, used, had tears shed on it, was made or given with love, and perhaps was being used when tragedy struck. 'Through my hands I keep part of these people alive, the way pearls glow with being worn.'

Our lace pincushion was inspired by a piece of antique lace and is worked simply and effectively in stranded cotton.

Approximate time needed: 18 hours
Finished size of design: 12 x 12 cm (4¾ x 4¾ in)
Yarns

Key	Anchor	Stranded Cotton	Skeins
A	926	Cream	3
B	366	Peach	2
C	392	Beige	4

Canvas
18-gauge white mono de luxe
Size: 17 x 17 cm (6¾ x 6¾ in)

Other materials
Tapestry needle, size 22
Ruler or tape measure
Masking tape for binding the canvas
Sharp scissors for cutting the canvas
Embroidery scissors
Sharp HB pencil or fine permanent marker
Eraser

Following the chart
Cut the canvas to the size given above and bind
the raw edges with masking tape to prevent
fraying. The design does not have to be marked
out on the canvas; just follow the color chart on
the opposite page. Remember that the squares
represent the canvas intersections, not the
holes. Each square represents one tent stitch.

The chart is divided into units of 10 squares by
10 squares to make it easier to follow. Before
beginning to stitch, it may be helpful to mark
your canvas in similar units of 10 squares by 10
squares with a sharp HB pencil or permanent
marker in a suitable color. Also, we suggest
marking the top of the canvas so that, if you turn
the canvas while stitching, you will still know
where the top is.

The colors on the chart are shown stronger
than the actual yarn colors to make them easier to
see. The corresponding yarns are given in the
color key below.

Stitches used
TENT stitch (1) has been used throughout. For
the stitch instructions, see page 90.

Stitching the design
Use the whole thread (six strands) of stranded
cotton throughout. Make sure you leave a border
of unstitched canvas around all the edges of the
design for stretching purposes. Begin stitching in
any area of canvas you wish. It might be easiest to
start at the top right hand corner 4–5 cm
(1½–2 in) in from the corner, working
horizontally from one block of color to another.

Making up instructions
When the design has been sewn, the needlepoint
may need to be stretched back into shape (see
stretching instructions on page 91). Then make it
up into a frilled pincushion as shown on page 92.

Key
A B C

TEAPOTS ☙

Wherever your tea-making skills lie, whether nearer the Japanese tea ceremony than the mad-hatter's tea party, most of us remember the best cup of tea we ever had, and have a childhood memory of a favorite cup, saucer or teapot. The history of tea and teapots is a fascinating one, and the equipment which etiquette required for making tea in the eighteenth century makes the subject rich in collectables. Teapot collections are very easy to begin because antique markets are often rich with such ubiquitous objects, although use and fragility mean that many more are lost than are saved.

Most collectors specialize, perhaps dictated by provenance, pedigree or just plain appeal. There are countless teapot collections with some of the most stunning gathered by American collectors, but the most staggering must surely be Edward Bramah's. His collection became so large it now forms the basis of the Tea and Coffee Museum at Butler's Wharf near London's Tower Bridge, where, at its peak over 300 years ago, 6,000 chests of tea were handled a day.

Edward Bramah says 'Banking is a business, oil is industry, tea and coffee are trades, but the tea trade in particular has always had a special aristocratic position in the world of buying and selling'. He believes the great tragedy in the history of tea has been television advertising, firstly for the rise in popularity of soluble coffee, secondly because short commercial breaks resulted in the advent of quick-brew, and subsequently the tea-bag and 'there is no romance about tea-bags, whereas there is a hidden social history of tea in a teapot'.

In the seventeenth century the Dutch introduced tea to Europe, from Macau on the China coast, where they had been imbibing the brew for 5,000 years. Bow, in London's East End, was called New Canton and the first Red Ware teapots were also made in London. It was the marriage of the Industrial Revolution, the Ellers brothers from Holland and the potteries at Stoke-on-Trent that created techniques to produce bone china and creamware, encouraged by the popularity for tea as the first hot, non-alcoholic drink. Tea became popular up and down the social ladder. For miners, farmers, factory and millworkers, green as well as black tea, with milk and sugar, became a refreshing food. For the middle classes, serving tea provided an opportunity to show off good manners. Spectacular Tea and Leisure Gardens were opened in the vicinity of London's fresh water springs, and became the pinnacle of social elegance. The phenomena of afternoon tea was born.

In the Bramah teapot collection, the pots line the walls and jostle each other for showcase space. And what teapots: satsuma, cloisonné, barge teapots with celebratory mottos, Minton teapots, transfer-printed, hand-painted, salt-glazed, silver, china stoneware, dragons and faces and flowers, animals, scenes, figures, majolica, japanesque, Victorian, commemorative, inventive (two spouts, three spouts) tea-kettles, caddies, crinolines, cosies, deco, miniatures, lustered, lead-glazed, gilded and porcelain . . . even the silver teapot belonging to the Scottish mother of Earl Grey (he of the China tea flavored with bergamot). As well as being functional, they are an insight into a procession of decorative styles.

Approximate time needed: 25 hours
Finished size of design: 16 cm (6¼ in) diameter
Yarns

Key	Anchor	Tapisserie Wool	Skeins
A	8814	Pale blue	1
B	8672	Mid-blue	1
C	8674	Dark blue	2
D	8120	Yellow	1
E	8100	Ocher	2
F	9536	Orange	1
G	8238	Red	1
H	9494	Chestnut	1
I	9674	Heather	1
J	8988	Emerald	1
K	8638	Navy	2

Canvas
14-gauge white mono de luxe
Size: 26 x 26 cm (10¼ x 10¼ in)
Other materials
Tapestry needle, size 20
Ruler or tape measure
Masking tape for binding the canvas
Sharp scissors for cutting the canvas
Embroidery scissors
Sharp HB pencil or fine permanent marker
Eraser

Following the chart
Cut canvas to size and bind edges with tape. The design does not have to be marked out on the canvas; just follow the chart opposite. The squares represent the canvas intersections, not the holes. Each square represents one tent stitch.

 The chart is divided into units of 10 squares by 10 squares to make it easier to follow. Before stitching, it may be helpful to mark your canvas in similar units of 10 squares by 10 squares with a pencil or permanent marker in a suitable color. Also, we suggest marking the top of the canvas so that if you turn the canvas while stitching you still know where the top is.

Stitches used
TENT stitch (1), STEM stitch (2) (optional). For the stitch instructions, see page 90.

Stitching the design
Use the whole thread of tapisserie wool throughout. Begin in any area you wish. It might be easiest to start at the top right hand corner 4–5 cm (1½–2 in) in from the corner of the canvas, working horizontally from one block of color to another. We have used STEM stitch (2) to outline the navy curved lines on either side of the border but this is optional. STEM stitch should be done after the TENT stitch areas are complete. Refer to the photograph of the teapot stand for the position of the STEM stitch.

Making up instructions
When the design has been sewn, the needlepoint may need to be stretched back into shape (see page 91). Then make it up into a teapot stand. Glorafilia can supply the teapot stand used here. Alternatively, you can use extra yarn and make it square if you cannot find a round frame to fit it, or a professional framer could stretch and frame it for you.

Key
A B C D E F G H I J K

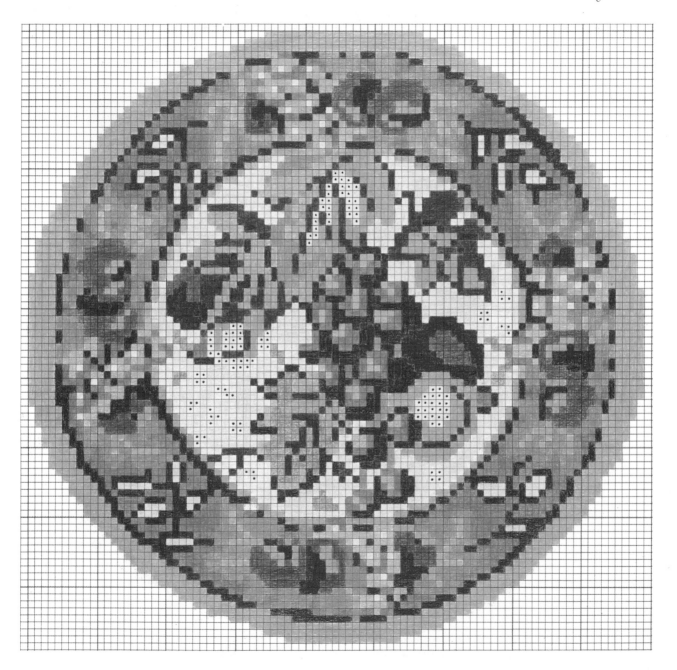

BAGS AND PURSES ❦

Anne Fortescue can't remember playing with her mother's handbags as a child, but can remember being fascinated with her jewellery, laying an aesthetic groundwork that no amount of time later in life can imitate. Later, involved in the antique business and particularly vintage clothes, she bought a petit-point bag. When she realized it was hand-made, she was captivated, and began buying bags whenever and wherever she saw them. She is only interested in European bags and prefers to buy bags perfect, but occasionally will have them relined, refringed, or re-set on an alternative frame.

Her bags are beautiful . . . beaded fringes fold onto the hand like cool chainmail; misers' purses either crocheted or made of metal beads, double ended with rings to keep small change; drawstring pouches with silky tassels; a sequined purse designed to contain a love letter, emblazoned with the words *je brule pour vous* (I burn for you); crocodile bags, strange shaped and oddly opening bags, fine antelope bags with compact interiors, enamel mesh, floral, geometric, bugle beads, seed pearls and crystal . . . she buys anything that has a direct appeal to her, be it eighteenth, nineteenth or twentieth century.

One American collector who has 900 bags ascertains the age of potential purchases with a magnet, lest the metal beads be aluminum and not steel. Most of us would be less purist, and use the 'heart-stop' technique! It's easy to appreciate why bags are so collectable – as most of them are made by hand they are seldom duplicated. And there is something quite special and sentimental about an item that has been used and handled.

Bags were first used in the twelfth century by men, and since that time have been an important item of costume. However, it is only since the late eighteenth century that bags have been used for carrying money. In general, transactions were achieved through barter, and servants' wages were paid annually, so a woman rarely needed money of her own – only the odd coin for the alms box. Perhaps in the future we shall revert, with just a credit card bonded to thumb and forefinger.

As women today, we joke about what we carry in our handbags, but in the 1600s a bag, worn under clothes, concealed such essentials as a hand-warmer and a container for rum. When aprons became fashionable, they were commodious enough to carry mirror and comb, smelling salts and knives, toothpicks, kerchiefs, pomanders, medicines, religious relics, keys and documents. Bags as we know them became fashionable when a graceful silhouette was desired and clothes could no longer accommodate them – the reticule, a gathered pouch usually closed with a drawstring, was feminine and charming, and served the purpose perfectly. Many beaded bags were made by the demure ladies of the Victorian middle-class, and periodicals would present a 'bag of the month', perhaps suggesting a London store for all materials.

The only bag that Anne has kept and refuses to sell is worked in 'micro-point' – the finest finest stitches – creating cherubs, figures, a fabulous garden (partly shown bottom right in the photograph). She feels it has 'everything'. Our roses evening bag was inspired by an antique piece from the nineteenth century, worked with a similar metallic gold background.

Approximate time needed: 32 hours
Finished size of design: 16 x 20 cm (6¼ x 7¾ in)

Yarns

Key	Anchor	Stranded Cotton	Skeins
A	301	Yellow	2
B	891	Gold	2
C	901	Ocher	2
D	375	Dark ocher	2
E	1009	Cream	2
F	376	Bois de rose	2
G	379	Marron	2
H	936	Dark marron	2
I	968	Pale pink	2
J	895	Rose	2
K	896	Dark rose	2
L	360	Chocolate	2
M	168	Turquoise	1
N	169	Peacock	1
O	267	Grass green	1
P	879	Bottle green	3
		Mez Astrella Metallic Thread	
Q	300	Gold	12

Canvas

18-gauge white mono de luxe
Size: 26 x 30 cm (10¼ x 11¾ in)

Other materials

Tapestry needle, size 22
Ruler or tape measure
Masking tape for binding the canvas
Sharp scissors for cutting the canvas
Embroidery scissors
Sharp HB pencil or fine permanent marker
Eraser
If the handle you choose has a bag attached to it, you can make a pattern from this; if not, make a pattern from brown paper and lay the handle along the top. You will see which shape looks right. The yarn quantities are for both sides.

Following the chart

Cut canvas to size and bind edges with tape. The design does not have to be marked out on the canvas; just follow the chart opposite. The squares represent the canvas intersections, not the holes. Each square represents one tent stitch.

The chart is divided into units of 10 squares by 10 squares to make it easier to follow. Before stitching, it may help to mark your canvas in similar units with a pencil or permanent marker. Mark the top of the canvas so that if you turn the canvas while stitching you know where the top is.

Stitches used

TENT stitch (1) has been used throughout. For the stitch instructions see page 90.

Stitching the design

The whole thread (six strands) of stranded cotton and one thread of Astrella gold have been used throughout. Begin in any area you wish. It might be easiest to start at the top right-hand corner 4–5 cm (1½–2 in) in from the corner, working horizontally from one block of color to another.

Making up instructions

When the design has been sewn, the needlepoint may need to be stretched back into shape (see page 91). If you follow our idea and make it into a bag using an antique frame, you will need to attach the needlepoint to the frame and line it with gold moire. For this, you will need 25 cm (10 in) of moire or similar for lining the bag and braid to finish the inside of the bag.

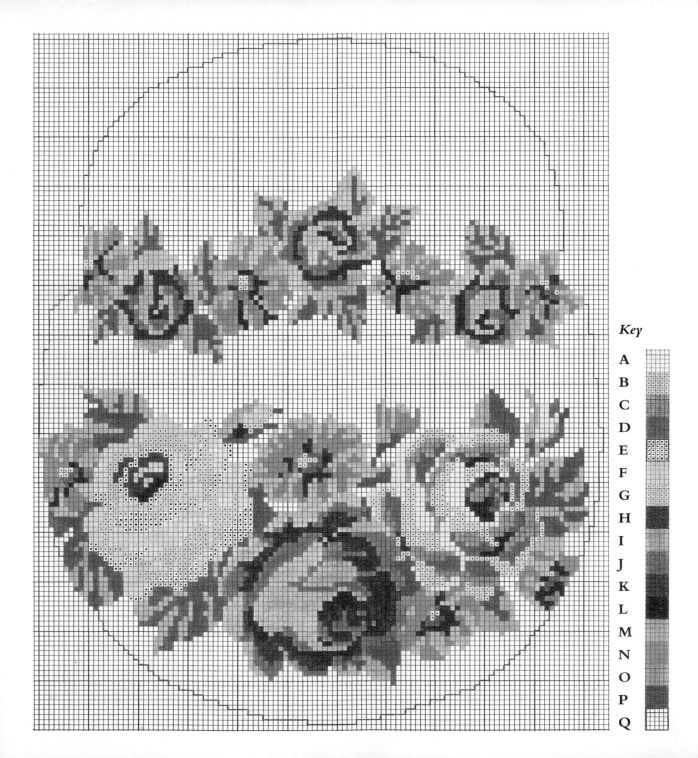

Key

A
B
C
D
E
F
G
H
I
J
K
L
M
N
O
P
Q

ANTIQUARIAN BOOKS &

Ah, books. To us, one of the ultimate desirables. Some of us are besotted by, others can take or leave alone. One sniff of an old binding, the tissue pages, gold edges that rub off on the fingers, embossing, fading inscriptions, can have an intoxicating effect on book lovers. There is a language to old books . . . crimson morocco with edges worn; silk-covered slip case (a little grubby); old limp vellum, edges rubbed, margins a little thumbed; speckled calf, upper corner nibbled (by what? A speckled calf? A bookworm?).

The collection we photographed began with a book on London's history, a subject that appears foremost in the collection, which then branches off in allied directions. The walls of the house are full of tantalizing books, their covers like secret doors. They formally and informally compete with netsukes, fossils, spearheads, panoramas (unrolling views on paper scrolls in beautiful boxes). Starting with a subject is the best way, because inevitably new avenues lead from the original, ad infinitum. Some bibliophiles collect subjects, some collect bindings or illustrators, then refinements like type-face or publisher. This particular collector remembers as a child collecting . . . cheese labels. (What joy! Another cheese label collector. Our mothers must have shopped at the same delicatessen!)

What makes a person a bibliophile? One impassioned collector of first editions claims it was childhood influences. His father was an omnivorous reader and books became a large part of life – he even remembers using books as building blocks. He was irreversibly steeped in books from the earliest age. In student days, when many of us walked around with a sensitive little volume of Hesse or Camus as the essential accessory, he read the major twentieth century novelists. When he started to earn money it seemed a natural progression to acquire better editions. He began collecting, scouring second-hand bookshops, and today owns a study full of his favorite things: first editions.

He has no interest in their value: he simply loves books as objects – his overwhelming reason for collecting is that to him there is nothing better than books – inscribed, plates pasted in, handled, a tangible piece of the past. Often there is the added charm of noting a piece of social history. For example, when Waugh's glorious *Brideshead Revisited* was published in 1945, it ignored the war's food shortages and extravagantly described six-course meals, which subsequent editions toned down.

Our needlepoint project, worked in a marbled design, is reminiscent of the endpapers found in antiquarian books. We remember a weekend in the country, spending most of the time in a marvellous second-hand bookshop, where the back rooms had shelves of books two or three deep, and magical walls that opened to reveal more shelves of yet more books and a large bureau with glass doors housing crumbling and powdery tomes. And where, overnight, the owner lovingly repaired the frayed spines of books we bought.

Once bitten, a bibliophile never loses the desire to collect another volume, and another. And he will also be heard to say: 'I regard this as the thing I treasure most of all – the privilege to be able to buy books'.

Approximate time needed for both: 35 hours

Finished size of design: Spectacle case 10 x 19 cm (3¾ x 7½ in)

Bookmark 5 x 21 cm (2 x 8 in)

Yarns

These quantities are for both projects. If you stitch just one, buy half the quantity of yarn.

Key	Anchor	Stranded Cotton	Skeins
A	926	Ivory	2
B	349	Russet	2
C	20	Red	2
D	206	Almond	3
E	8581	Taupe	2
F	847	Pale gray	2
G	848	Pale marine blue	2
H	850	Mid marine blue	2
I	979	Kingfisher	2
J	401	Charcoal	2

Canvas

18-gauge white mono de luxe

Size: 20 x 29 cm (7¾ x 11½ in) spectacle case

15 x 31 cm (6 x 12 in) bookmark

Other materials

Tapestry needle, size 22

Ruler or tape measure

Masking tape for binding the canvas

Sharp scissors for cutting the canvas

Embroidery scissors

Sharp HB pencil or fine permanent marker

Eraser

Following the chart

Cut the canvas to size and bind the edges with masking tape. The design does not have to be marked on the canvas; just follow the color chart opposite. Remember that the squares represent the canvas intersections, not the holes. Each square represents one tent stitch.

The chart is divided into units of 10 squares by 10 squares to make it easier to follow. Before beginning to stitch, it may be helpful to mark your canvas in similar units of 10 squares by 10 squares with an HB pencil or permanent marker in a suitable color. Also, we suggest marking the top of the canvas so that if you turn the canvas while stitching you know where the top is.

The colors on the chart are shown stronger than the actual yarn colors to make them easier to see. The corresponding yarns are given in the color key.

Stitches used

TENT stitch (1) has been used throughout. For the stitch instructions, see page 90.

Stitching the design

Use the whole thread (six strands) of stranded cotton throughout. Begin in area you wish. It might be easiest to start at the top right hand corner of the canvas, 4–5 cm (1½–2 in) in from the corner, working horizontally from one block of color to another.

Making up instructions

After sewing, the needlepoint may need to be stretched back into shape (see page 91). Then follow the making up instructions on page 92.

Key

A
B
C
D
E
F
G
H
I
J

TENNIS MEMORABILIA 🎾

Some collectors gather myriad objects that tumble over each other, shelves full, cupboards stuffed, acquired in paroxysms of possessiveness. Some have misconceptions of what they already own, and are surprised when taking home a new acquisition to find its twin lurking in a corner (the 'I-know-someone-who-has-that-piece-oh-it's-me' syndrome, not unfamiliar among compulsives). However, Sally King, whose tennis memorabilia we show, collects with military discipline. No sloppy indecision or blurred edges for her, gaps in collections are filled, everything exquisitely grouped and displayed, not the hodge-podge of ephemera it is easy to become prey to.

Sally believes that if you are a born collector, it doesn't matter what you collect. It is the hunt, the sniff of the chase – antique fairs where the chance sighting of a particular handle or glaze can send the adrenalin soaring and the heart racing far quicker than a bid at Sothebys. She collected stamps as a child (and still does) and Elvis ephemera and has graduated to exquisite enamel boxes, perfume bottles, Moorcroft and Dalton miniatures. With her vast collection of photographs she also collects memories.

Tennis is the most recent addition of collectables and fills a tennis pavilion with energy and elegance, wit and flamboyance. The majority of the collection is figurative: in bronze, porcelain or spelter, charming players from the nineteenth century, daintily wielding their racquets. Of all racquet games, it was only tennis that enjoyed such social connections: from tennis on the lawn, it was a short step to tea on the lawn, with appropriate tea-services and racquet-shaped teaspoons, toast racks, trays, gongs and from there into other elegant enthusiasts' paraphernalia: ink stands, letter racks, parlor games, bookends, ornaments in general. Then as now, the social side of tennis was sometimes as important as the game itself.

Her collection depicts tennis as an elite pastime: genteel, romantic, leisured. With the first woman to win Wimbledon wearing an elaborate bustle, a straw boater and black stockings, imagine how the less-streamlined society players dressed! Tennis inspired a multitude of pictorial images, in posters, prints, cartoons and cigarette cards, helping us to imagine the atmosphere of the epoque, which we hope is shown in our 1920s' style needlepoint picture.

Real, or royal, tennis was played in France a thousand years ago, when the first racket used was the hand (the game is still called *jeu de paume*). Rackets were introduced in the 1500s, and since then there have been many variations and refinements. These provide a wealth of collectables and interesting information – for example, it took the intestines of seven sheep to string one racket (cats and their guts have nothing to do with it!).

Sally agrees with the opinion that collecting stems from an insecurity, the need many of us have to surround ourselves with an armour of possessions, and thinks we should blame childhood deprivations! She says, 'Like an addiction, it's the anticipation of finding a new piece, the build-up, the negotiating, and the possession. It feeds you at that moment. The new piece is absorbed into the collection, and you're after the next one'.

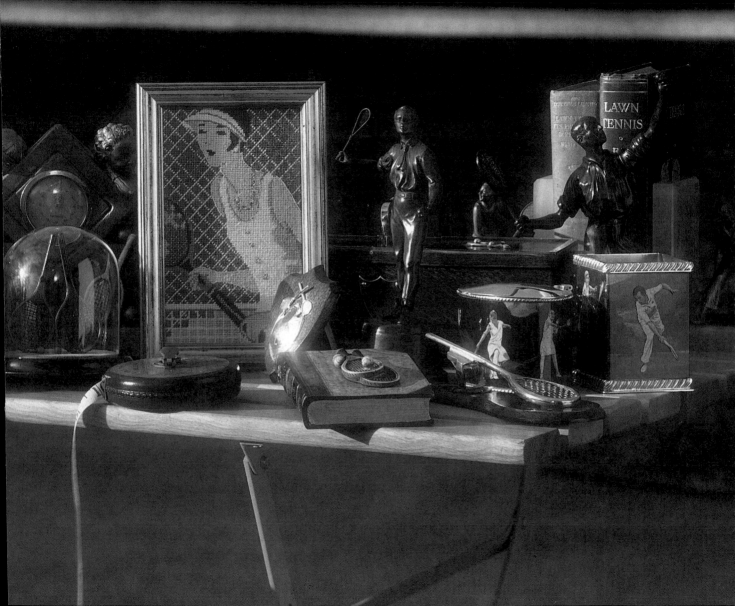

Approximate time needed: 40 hours
Finished size of design: 12 x 19 cm (4½ x 7½ in)
Yarns

Key	Anchor	Stranded Cotton	Skeins
A	926	Ecru	4
B	216	Green	4
C	398	Gray	1
D	830	Beige	1
E	46	Red	1
F	378	Fawn	1
G	371	Chestnut	1
H	881★	Flesh	2
	Mez Reflecta		
I	0300	Gold	2

Canvas

18-gauge white mono deluxe
Size: 22 x 29 cm (8½ x 11½ in)

Other materials

Tapestry needle, size 22
Ruler or tape measure
Masking tape for binding the canvas
Sharp scissors for cutting the canvas
Embroidery scissors
Sharp HB pencil or fine permanent marker
Eraser

Following the chart

Cut the canvas to size and bind the edges with masking tape. The design does not have to be marked out on the canvas; just follow the color chart opposite. Remember that the squares represent the canvas intersections, not the holes. Each square represents one tent stitch.

The chart is divided into units of 10 squares by 10 squares to make it easier to follow. Before stitching, it may be helpful to mark your canvas in similar units with an HB pencil or permanent marker in a suitable color. Mark the top of the canvas so that if you turn the canvas while stitching you know where the top is.

The colors on the chart are shown stronger than the actual yarn colors to make them easier to see. The corresponding yarns are given in the color key.

Stitches used

TENT stitch (1), STEM stitch (2) (optional). For the stitch instructions, see page 90.

Stitching the design

Use the whole thread (six strands) of stranded cotton throughout with the exception of the outlining where three strands have been used. Three strands of the gold thread have also been used. Begin with TENT stitch (1) in any area you wish. It might be easiest to start at the top right hand corner of the canvas, 4–5 cm (1½–2 in) in from the corner, working horizontally from one block of color to another.

We have used STEM stitch (2) to outline her arms and hands, face and nose, neck, armhole of her dress and her beads. If you decide to use STEM stitch, this should be done after the TENT stitch areas are complete. Refer to the photograph of the finished picture for the position of the STEM stitch.

Making up instructions

Many needlepointers feel experienced enough to stretch and make up their needlepoint designs, but we always feel that a needlepoint should be framed by a professional experienced in stretching and framing needlepoint.

Key

A

B

C

D

E

F

G

★H

★★H

I

Note★
We have shown 881 on the chart in two different colors to enable you to see the STEM stitch outlining more clearly. STEM stitch is the second color ★★.

THE FROG COLLECTION ℰ

Sheila Crown collects frogs, any kind except real frogs. The exclusive and the kitsch stand shoulder to shoulder, buttock by jowl. She has over five thousand, meticulously cataloged, room by room, and cabinet by cabinet, and table by window ledge and lawn by terrace. When asked if she has favorites, she lifts a perfect eyebrow and replies 'Of course. I really can't be attached to *all* those frogs!'.

She has a nose for frogs. Her plane stopped in Antigua to refuel and she managed to find a kiosk with a frog for sale. She admits she passes through normal phases and what you could call 'obsessive' phases, and acknowledges that there is an amazing number of people who collect in this extraordinary way.

After its size, the striking thing about the collection is its humor. All right, all right, frogs are not 'Serious Stuff', but the breadth of style and wit is astonishing, from the 'Warning – Frogs Crossing' road-sign outside the house and croaking door chimes, past the Lalique, Picasso and neon frogs, out to the waterfall leaping with happy froggies in stone, lead and bronze.

Like most collectors, Sheila has always collected something: dolls, china animals, rabbits as a child. Her daughter, by her instigation, has developed the collecting code: fans, thimbles. Sheila 'fell into frogs', needing an ornament for a green study. Then another. And fired by a visit to a Dutch frog collector, and on the basis of 'more than one of anything is a collection' began collecting in earnest. If duplication happens, she'll swap, or give it away, it will never be added to the frog log. Her intention is to achieve the world's largest frog collection, and she cannot be far off reaching her goal.

It seems that every room overflows with frogs: there are mirror frogs, musical frogs, artes nouveau and deco, mosaic, miniature and gargantuan, ethnic frogs, gold, silver, ceramic and marcasite frogs, sporting and dancing frogs, crouching under the billiard table frogs, frogs disguised as chairs and lamps, cuddling frogs, erotic frogs, frogs masquerading as keyrings, candlesticks, bookends, frames, boxes. They are in wood, bronze and papier mâché, glass and iron, and sitting on floors, walls, window sills and every available surface. There are chess sets, masked frogs, velvet frogs, frogs erupting out of eggs, cast in porcelain and pewter, frogs by Royal Dalton, Majolica, and one frog prince. No warts.

For Sheila Crown, like most of the collectors in this book, it is quintessentially the pleasure of the hunt – knowing where to look, knowing the people who will quickly pass on a sighting, responding well to serendipity (can a chance meeting with a frog really be serendipitous?) and finessing the purchase, if necessary, with a poker face.

Our needlepoint frog, inspired by a South American frog from Sheila's collection, thought he was in quite exalted company, and puffed himself up to have his photograph taken with such a well-spawned group. Frogs have always had a rather bad press, and could do with some image lifting. From the ghastly Kermit to Aristophanes' immortal frog chorus, frogs usually have to hide their light under a lilypad. And unfairly, for surely a creature so painted and sculpted must have amazing charisma?

Approximate time needed: 30 hours
Finished size of design: 18 x 26 cm (7 x 10 in)
Yarns

Key	Anchor	Tapisserie Wool	Skeins
A	9258	Green	2
B	9532	Apricot	1
C	9556	Orange	2
D	9512	Terracotta	1
E	9562	Rust	1
F	9386	Beige	4
G	9292	Brown	3

Canvas
14-gauge white mono de luxe
Size: 28 x 36 cm (11 x 14 in)

Other materials
Tapestry needle, size 20
Ruler or tape measure
Masking tape for binding the canvas
Sharp scissors for cutting the canvas
Embroidery scissors
Sharp HB pencil or fine permanent marker
Eraser

Following the chart
Cut the canvas to size and bind the edges with masking tape. The design does not have to be marked out on the canvas; just follow the color chart opposite. Remember that the squares represent the canvas intersections, not the holes. Each square represents one tent stitch.

The chart is divided into units of 10 squares by 10 squares to make it easier to follow. Before stitching, it may be helpful to mark your canvas in similar units with an HB pencil or permanent marker in a suitable color. Also, we suggest marking the top of the canvas so that, if you turn the canvas while stitching, you know where the top is.

The colors on the chart are shown stronger than the actual yarn colors to make them easier to see. The corresponding yarns are given in the color key.

Stitches used
TENT stitch (1) is used throughout. For stitch instructions see page 90.

Stitching the design
Use the whole thread of tapisserie wool throughout. Begin with TENT stitch (1) in any area you wish. It might be easiest to start at the top right hand corner 4–5 cm (1½–2 in) in from the corner of the canvas, working horizontally from one block of color to another.

Making up instructions
When the design has been sewn, the needlepoint may need to be stretched back into shape (see page 91). Then make it up into a shaped cushion.

You will need 25 cm (10 in) felt, pins and terylene/kapok.

After you have stretched the frog back into shape, make a paper pattern by tracing around the edge of your sewn frog. Cut out the felt, adding 1 cm (½ in) all around for seams. The design should also be cut out leaving a 1 cm (½ in) border of unsewn canvas. With right sides together, tack the felt to the tapestry, sewing as close to the design as possible. Then machine or back stitch, leaving an opening of approximately 7.5 cm (3 in). Turn back to the right side and stuff with terylene or kapok. Finally, using slip stitch, close the opening.

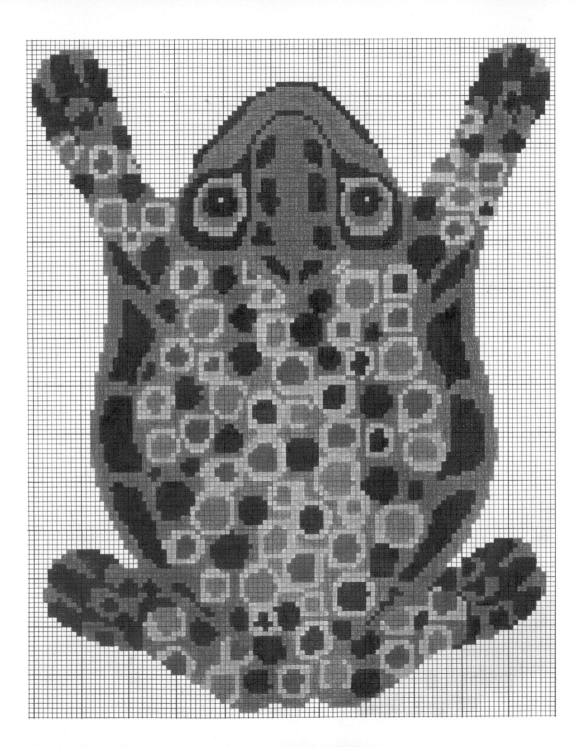

Key

A
B
C
D
E
F
G

PERFUME BOTTLES ₹

Since the time of the ancient Egyptians, small decorative jars have been used as containers for perfume, and perfume itself used since the human desire for self-adornment, and the instinct to beautify, reared its head. Over the centuries incense was used for religious ceremonies, scents were worn to protect against contagious diseases, aromatic herbs were used by apothecaries. Exotic spices were added to herbs, and pomanders and nosegays were carried in the belief that they would keep away evil smells and disease.

Cosmetics became fashionable from the 1700s, but it wasn't until this century that commercial perfume bottles were manufactured. Prior to that perfume would be bought in plain containers and decanted into the customer's own decorative bottle. Small companies made perfumes, and books were published giving the recipes. One of our daughters has a perfume bottle collection, begun by an indulgent uncle, with bottles so beautiful they spoil her for anything less, her eye from a very young age developing a depressingly extravagant point of reference. The collection includes a small leather case of phials with names on faded labels: Victoire, Lune de Miel, Goutte d'Or, Jeunesse Dorée, Jasmine del Pais, still smelling with an intensity that catches in the throat, redolent of remembrances of things past. As with the antique dolls that were played with under nanny's watchful eye, she only rarely and gingerly took them from their cabinet, and handled them with awe (and two accidents).

It is not only the huge variety that makes perfume bottles fascinating to collect: they are extremely beautiful and tactile, some surprisingly heavy and robust. There is marvellous faceting, mouth-watering colors like sapphire, cranberry, turquoise and emerald, clear or opaline, hand-painted porcelain, enamels; some decorated with gold, some with intricately worked silver stoppers. Collectors may also find themselves seduced by double-ended bottles, intended for both smelling salts and perfume – the smelling-salts end has a wider neck to allow the fumes to be inhaled more easily, by (literally) straight-laced and oxygen-starved Victorian ladies needing a quick sniff of something reviving. Perfume bottles, on the other hand, have a narrow neck to prevent scent evaporating. There are also vinaigrettes, containing sponge soaked in perfume or vinegar, held in place behind a grill, and worn to ward off fumes of sewage-strewn streets, as well as smells of a more personal nature.

The 1880s were a time of the greatest invention and exuberance in bottle design, followed by the turn-of-the-century French, providing us with some of the all-time stunning examples. The glassmaker Emile Gallé, influenced by the Chinese, worked in cameo glass with opaque and semi-translucent effects. And it's appropriate that René Lalique, with his incomparable frosted and opalescent glass, made his first foray into glass with perfume bottles.

Our needlepoint project is a small sachet stuffed with pot pourri. It was inspired by nineteenth century Bohemian glass phials, tapered as pencils, faceted and gilded. Each panel shows a different style of decoration of these exquisite little bottles. The colour is like ruby glass, worked in fine silver and cotton threads.

Approximate time needed: 24 hours

Finished size of design: 13 x 13 cm (5 x 5 in)

Yarns

Key	Anchor	Stranded Cotton	Skeins
A	275	White	2
B	1027	Cranberry	6
	Mez Ophir		
C	301	Silver	1

Canvas

18-gauge white mono de luxe

Size: 23 x 23 cm (9 x 9 in)

Other materials

Tapestry needle, size 22

Ruler or tape measure

Masking tape for binding the canvas

Sharp scissors for cutting the canvas

Embroidery scissors

Sharp HB pencil or fine permanent marker

Eraser

Following the chart

Cut the canvas to size and bind the edges with masking tape. The design does not have to be marked out on the canvas; just follow the color chart opposite. Remember that the squares represent the canvas intersections, not the holes. Each square represents one TENT stitch.

The chart is divided into units of 10 squares by 10 squares to make it easier to follow. Before stitching, it may be helpful to mark your canvas in similar units with an HB pencil or permanent marker in a suitable color. Also, we suggest marking the top of the canvas so that, if you turn the canvas while stitching, you know where the top is.

The colors on the chart are shown stronger than the actual yarn colors to make them easier to see. The corresponding yarns are given in the color key.

Stitches used

TENT stitch (1), COUCHING stitch (3) (optional). We have used COUCHING for the silver lines that divide the panels. For the stitch instructions, see page 90.

Stitching the design

The whole thread (six strands) of stranded cotton and two strands of silver thread have been used. Begin with TENT stitch in any area you wish. It might be easiest to start at the top right hand corner 4–5 cm (1½–2 in) in from the corner of the canvas, working horizontally from one block of color to another. If you decide to do the COUCHING, do this last. Where the vertical silver lines appear to divide the sections, work the lines first in TENT stitch (1) in cranberry stranded cotton. Then lay one line of silver thread (two strands) along the length of the needlepoint from the top to the bottom, positioning it between the stitches as shown on the chart and catch it down every 1 cm (½ in) with a tiny stitch to hold it in place.

Making up instructions

When the design has been sewn, the needlepoint may need to be stretched back into shape (see page 91). Make up into a sachet as on page 92.

Key

A B C

AGATE JEWELRY &

When Queen Victoria declared enthusiasm for all things Scottish, draped Balmoral Castle and her children in tartan, the country followed suit. Visiting Scotland's romantic scenery, and enjoying its culture and tradition became very fashionable. Tourists wanted souvenirs, and by 1870 it is thought there were a thousand craftsmen involved in satisfying the rage for 'Scottish' jewelry – the huge brooches that secured tartan at the shoulder, the decorative daggers, skean dhu, all made from stones from the local banks, braes and burns. Canny jewellers using the same techniques as the Scots leapt on the bandwagon and began producing all the forms of jewelry the Victorians loved: bracelets, brooches, buckles, necklaces, earrings.

Scottish jewelry traditionally used agates in glorious variety: dense and flecked, banded in stripes, milky and cloud-like; granites of pink and gray, transparent citrines and amethyst, red cornelian, dark green and scarlet bloodstone, jaspers. The simplicity of the Scottish stones was augmented with agates from India, Africa and Germany, and the brilliant mineral green of malachite from Siberia. And while traditional jewellers in Scotland continued to craft their classic pieces, 'Scottish' jewelry became international.

These pieces of jewelry have all the elements that epitomize the unique character of Scotland: the mix of lyricism and precision, subtlety and strength, miraculous shapes and colors, abstract and solid, whimsical and iron-fisted – even flamboyant and unpretentious at the same time . . . all this is there in the agate jewelry.

The first sight of Brian and Lynn Holmes' agates is absolutely arresting. Instead of being neatly arranged as with conventional jewelry, the agates are bold and tumbling in brilliant discord and pattern, polished stone with minutely engraved silver, swirling celtic shapes and dazzling colors.

Lynn Holmes collects agate spectacularly. From the instant she saw celtic jewelry over twenty years ago she realized the magic of these pieces is that they are 'unprecious', and still wonderful. She agrees it is definitely an acquired taste, because some of the pieces are ridiculously theatrical, and talks lyrically of never becoming bored with them because the colors and strata are unrepeatable.

Much of the charm of collecting these beautiful pieces is that they are extremely wearable – not for these the fate of being kept under lock and key or brought out periodically for an airing, like a fragile relative. Unlike 'high' jewelry, these can be worn casually or formally, to ignite dour colors, for walking through heather, or a quick highland fling. Jennifer has been collecting, and wearing, celtic jewelry for years and claims, sensibly, that you can never have too many pieces. Her first piece was a brooch that she was just drawn to, not realizing this would be the start of the slippery slope.

Our needlepoint project is a jewelry roll, inspired by diamond shapes on an agate brooch, made around 1880. Each section is divided by a silver strip, and with the superb mineral colors of jasper, malachite and cornelian. Worked on a large gauge canvas in appropriate wool, the design repeated once, this would make a superb cushion.

Approximate time needed: 45 hours
Finished size of design: 21 x 31 cm (8 x 12 in)
Yarns

Key	Anchor	Stranded Cotton	Skeins
A	387	Cream	1
B	403	Black	3
C	891	Pale yellow	2
D	890	Gold	3
E	349	Caramel	3
F	352	Chestnut	2
G	341	Rust	3
H	398	Pale gray	2
I	939	Blue	2
J	400	Gunmetal	3
K	189	Emerald	2
L	212	Bottle green	2
M	683	Dark green	4
	Mez Ophir		*Spools*
N	301	Silver	2

Canvas
14-gauge white mono de luxe
Size: 31 x 41 cm (12 x 16 in)
Other materials
Tapestry needle, size 20
Ruler or tape measure
Masking tape for binding the canvas
Sharp scissors for cutting the canvas
Embroidery scissors
Sharp HB pencil or fine permanent marker
Eraser

Following the chart
Cut the canvas to size and bind the edges with masking tape. The design does not have to be marked out on the canvas; just follow the color chart opposite. Remember that the squares represent the canvas intersections, not the holes. Each square represents one TENT stitch.

The chart is repeated three times, working from the top down. The narrow top panel **A** appears only once at the beginning. Thereafter, **B** joins up with **C**. The quantities given are for three repeats, you could of course make it bigger or smaller.

The chart is divided into units of 10 squares by 10 squares to make it easier to follow. Before beginning to stitch, it may be helpful to mark your canvas in similar units of 10 squares by 10 squares with an HB pencil or permanent marker in a suitable color. Also, we suggest marking the top of the canvas so that, if you turn the canvas while stitching, you will still know where the top edge is.

The colors on the chart are shown stronger than the actual yarn colors to make them easier to see. The corresponding yarns are given in the color key.

Stitches used
TENT stitch (1), COUCHING stitch (3) (optional). We have used COUCHING for the silver lines that divide the diamonds. For the stitch instructions, see page 90.

Stitching the design
The whole thread (six strands) of stranded cotton and three strands of silver have been used throughout. Begin in any area you wish. It might be easiest to start at the top right hand corner, 4–5 cm (1½–2 in) in from the corner, working horizontally from one block of color to another. If you decide to COUCH the diamonds with silver thread (using three strands), do this after all

the TENT stitch is complete. Lay lengths of silver thread the full length of each side of each diamond, anchoring down this loose thread as you go, with tiny stitches every 5 mm (¼ in) — see the photograph for the position.

Making up instructions

When the design has been sewn, the needlepoint may need to be stretched back into shape (see stretching instructions on page 91). Then make it up into a jewelry roll as shown on page 93. Alternatively, this design could be adapted to make a stool or a cushion. Simply enlarge the design and use larger gauge canvas.

Key

A B C D E F G H I J K L M N

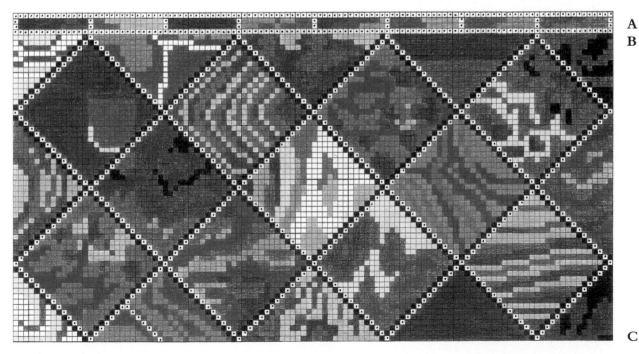

A
B

C

ANTIQUE DOLLS ❦

Of course, it can happen that a doll found in a garage sale fetches thousands at auction, but this is rare. Such dolls, in good condition, are generally treasured – though as long as there are unexplored attics, there will always be the possibility of undiscovered gold.

These special dolls rarely suffered the same fate as over-loved teddies. They were expensive even then, so handling them was usually only permitted under nanny's vigilant eye. And with a china head and appendages, sawdust or wood-stuffed bodies jointed with metal, they were also too heavy for any real 'playing'.

There is no comparison with today's dolls. It is now impossible to get the same minerals for paints or the bisques (the unglazed china clay that was used for head, feet and hands). David Barrington, whose magnificent collection of dolls we photographed, appreciates antique dolls as beautiful works of art, and looking at his astonishing collection, it's hard not to agree.

The period he most likes is from 1880 to 1900, particularly the French and German dolls with real charm and softness and eyes that follow you round the room. Their clothes would have been handmade, and he has dressmakers who replace clothes with fabrics from the period, perhaps from a lesser or broken doll. Fine dolls have giveaway marks: an imprint on the back of the neck, the not-quite-smooth feeling of the bisque, the beautifully sewn seams on the body. Of course the face is exquisitely modelled, and fingers and toes sculpted finely. And to the expert, they smell like a piece of history.

David began by being captivated by a doll in the window of an antique shop. Twenty years ago you could buy dolls easily and cheaply; he would fill his car with them and take them home to restore if necessary. That was his 'apprenticeship', getting to know and appreciate every last little bit of them; today it's harder to acquire such experience. He advises new collectors buying on their eye from local sales or antique fairs to beware of dolls looking too 'aged' – this isn't difficult to fake and a good doll, because it was treasured, will probably be quite clean.

The doll he says most new collectors want to own is 'Mein Leibling' produced by Kammer & Reinhardt from 1909 onwards. Many thousands were made and were broken, because by that time children were beginning to play with dolls. It embodies the idea of the perfect little girl – a pouty, turn of the century look, though from personal experience the dolls we gravitate to are those that ring memory bells for us. As years went on, dolls changed dramatically from beautiful 'pretend' ladies to children, and in Edwardian times were modelled on children from life.

David's shop is truly an experience. Turn slowly and a thousand aloof, surreal eyes watch you, with painted lashes, feathered brows. Coquettish cupid's bows part to show tiny porcelain or milk-glass teeth. Dimpled knuckles, frilled cuffs, regimented ankle boots. Not sure we'd be able to spend a night here!

Our doll portrait is worked in cotton to give her luminosity; her arched brows and delicate rosebud mouth give the serious expression typical of antique dolls.

Approximate time needed: 30 hours
Finished size of design: 14 x 18 cm (5½ x 7 in)
Yarns

Key	Anchor	Stranded Cotton	Skeins
A	Ecru	Pale flesh	3
B	778	Pale pink	1
C	868	Salmon	1
D	883	Terracotta	1
E	371	Chestnut	2
F	360	Chocolate	2
G	920	Blue	1
H	852	Buttermilk	2
I	853	Sand	2
J	888	Dark sand	2
K	969	Pale rose pink	1
L	970	Rose pink	1

Canvas

18-gauge white mono de luxe
Size: 24 x 28 cm (9½ x 11 in)

Other materials

Tapestry needle, size 22
Ruler or tape measure
Masking tape for binding the canvas
Sharp scissors for cutting the canvas
Embroidery scissors
Sharp HB pencil or fine permanent marker
Eraser

Following the chart

Cut the canvas to size and bind the edges with masking tape. The design does not have to be marked out on the canvas; just follow the color chart opposite. Remember that the squares represent the canvas intersections, not the holes. Each square represents one tent stitch.

The chart is divided into units of 10 squares by 10 squares to make it easier to follow. Before stitching, it may be helpful to mark your canvas in similar units with a pencil or permanent marker in a suitable color. Mark the top of the canvas so that if you turn the canvas while stitching you know where the top is.

The colors on the chart are shown stronger than the actual yarn colors to make them easier to see. The corresponding yarns are given in the color key.

Stitches used

TENT stitch (1), STEM stitch (2) (optional). For the stitch instructions, see page 90.

Stitching the design

Use the whole thread (six strands) of stranded cotton with the exception of any outlining when three strands should be used. Begin with TENT stitch (1) in any area you wish. It might be easiest to start at the top right hand corner 4–5 cm (1½–2 in) in from the corner of the canvas, working horizontally from one block of color to another. We have used STEM stitch to outline her hat, on the edge of her eyelids and around her chin, but this is optional. The STEM stitch should be done after the TENT stitch areas are complete. Refer to the photograph of the framed picture on page 55 for the position of the STEM stitch.

Making up instructions

Many needlepointers feel experienced enough to stretch and make up their needlepoint designs, but we always feel they should be framed by a professional experienced in stretching and framing needlepoint.

Key

A
B
C
D
E
F
G
H
I
J
K
L

TARTANWARE

Inland from Ayr, on the coast of Scotland, is the town of Mauchline. At the height of its success in the middle of the nineteenth century, hundreds of people were employed there manufacturing a fascinating range of wooden items, all made so exquisitely and with such a superb finish that they have become increasingly 'collected'. They all have something in common: they are small and useful and very beautiful.

Mauchline ware began with snuff boxes with an ingenious hidden hinge. However, snuff-taking declined and it was necessary to make new products, and our picture shows a few of these pieces . . . containers for string, for needles and scissors, book covers, glove stretchers, dance-programs, cotton-reel holders, stamp boxes, blotter, ruler, 'go-to-bed' (strike the match, place it in the little holder and it will stay alight just long enough to take off your slippers and get into bed), an egg cup, napkin rings, an ink well shaped like an egg and multiple charming little boxes, all with a designated purpose and in the tartan of a particular clan.

The tartans were originally painstakingly hand-painted onto the wood until a new technique for printing the designs onto paper was invented – and 69 'authentic' tartans were developed. Many of the shapes are curved, and the skill needed to apply and match the tartan paper was enormous. To avoid tucks, or mismatching the patterns, the joins were painted and disguised with a jagged gold line, and each clan name discreetly stamped onto the product.

We all use different expressions to describe that rush of adrenalin that accompanies finding something that excites us, that makes the heart stop and the pulse flutter. Noel Gibson, tartan authority extraordinaire, gets a 'buzz in the tummy'. His first tartan-related buzz came when he found a case full of tartanware rotting in a cellar. The contents were beyond restoration, but sparked something in his mind, anticipating the popularity of these pieces and the degree to which they were going to be prized.

A relative of Noel's wrote a biography of Sir Walter Scott, and he feels there must be something running through his veins that draws him to things Scottish: for many years he dealt in Celtic agate jewelry and he loves Scottish furniture. The tartanware is another link in the chain. He has his private collection of special pieces 'not necessarily the most expensive', and becomes quite lyrical over memories of a child's tartan slate, hidden hinges, satisfying shapes, and early hand-painted boxes, one with a particularly stunning steeplechase, another with a miniature portrait of Wellington. Such portraits are very desirable.

The photoframe in the picture is our needlepoint project, featuring our own hybrid tartan from Mill Hill. Like many people, we have a weakness for tartan (and Scotties, and bagpipes, and Scottish men with lilting voices) and one year produced a whole catalog of tartan needlepoint. For absolute accuracy, it is preferable to work a tartan pattern either from a hand-painted canvas or a chart such as this. Instead of leaving the space for a photograph or a favorite picture in the center, you could fill in with tent stitch and personalize it with initials and a date.

Approximate time needed: 22 hours
Finished size of design: 13.5 x 19 cm (5¼ x 7½ in)
Yarns

Key	Anchor	Stranded Cotton	Skeins
A	933	Ecru	1
B	403	Black	2
C	216	Light green	2
D	218	Dark green	2
E	872	Mauve	3
F	146	Blue	1
G	46	Red	4
H	891	Gold	1

Canvas
18-gauge white mono de luxe
Size: 23.5 x 29.5 cm (9¼ x 11½ in)

Other materials
Tapestry needle, size 22
Ruler or tape measure
Masking tape for binding the canvas
Sharp scissors for cutting the canvas
Embroidery scissors
Sharp HB pencil or fine permanent marker
Eraser

Following the chart
Cut the canvas to size and bind the edges with masking tape. The design does not have to be marked out on the canvas; just follow the color chart opposite. Remember that the squares represent the canvas intersections, not the holes. Each square represents one tent stitch.

The chart is divided into units of 10 squares by 10 squares to make it easier to follow. Before beginning to stitch, it may be helpful to mark your canvas in similar units of 10 squares by 10 squares with an HB pencil or permanent marker

in a suitable color. Also, we suggest marking the top of the canvas so that if you turn the canvas while stitching you will still know where the top edge is.

The colors on the chart are shown stronger than the actual yarn colors to make them easier to see. The corresponding yarns are given in the color key.

Stitches used
TENT stitch (1). For the stitch instructions, see page 90.

Stitching the design
Use the whole thread of stranded cotton (six strands) throughout. Begin with TENT stitch (1) in any area you wish. It might be easiest to start at the top right hand corner 4–5 cm (1½–2 in) in from the corner of the canvas, working horizontally from one block of color to another.

Making up instructions
Many needlepointers feel experienced enough to stretch and make up their needlepoint designs but we always feel that a photograph frame should be made up by a professional framer experienced in stretching and framing needlepoint.

Key

A
B
C
D
E
F
G
H

THIMBLES ET CETERA ℰ

Sewing accessories are so delightfully small that sometimes a lifetime's collection can be packed in a shoe box (unlike a collection of Victorian carved chairs or nineteenth century Indian columns. Enough said). Essentials for grooming, writing and shaving were often contained together in what is charmingly called a 'necessaire', and the smallest and daintiest necessaires were for sewing, intended to be hung from the chatelaine's waist.

Some sewing accessories sound like instruments of torture: stilettos, clamps, tambour hooks, Chinese sewing rings; others sound more friendly: waxers for waxing thread, winders made from mother-of-pearl, wood or bone, spool-boxes, emeries for cleaning rusty needles, shuttles, thimble guards, lucets for making cord – beautifully crafted, tactile little objects. Brings back fond memories of an antique Chinese needle case, borrowed permanently by the same daughter whose taste was sharpened by her perfume bottle collection, to hang round her neck.

On first seeing a collection of thimbles, the reaction may well be one of surprise. They are so varied, so interesting and so attractive. The word thimble probably originated from the medieval English thymel, meaning thumb, though the first 'needle pushers' go back to Neolithic times, developed to protect the hand while sewing. There is more and more knowledge surfacing about thimbles from archaeological digs, putting them at over a thousand years old, the earliest in bronze, iron and brass. Over the generations, thimbles became finer, with embroidery requiring a daintier thimble than one used for heavy

sailmaking. Needlework came to be regarded as an elegant activity for leisured ladies, and thimbles became more beautiful and a very acceptable gift, with silver first being introduced during the seventeenth century.

Some thimbles make a very inexpensive way of starting a collection – for example the aluminum advertising thimbles from the 1920s with bright slogan borders, which were often given as change instead of a farthing. Collectors usually specialize in a particular type: one Australian collector only wants town name thimbles. Worcester birds are very popular, finely painted on porcelain, as are the commemorative thimbles in Queen Victoria's reign, celebrating her coronation and various jubilees. Aesop's fables are depicted on silver thimbles; there are medieval acorn-shaped thimbles (for medieval acorn-shaped fingers?) and we love the bronze Hispano-Moresque thimbles dug up in southern Spain, evoking something from the crusades.

The style of thimble, shown centrally in the photograph, became very popular when it was used inside the Atlantic Telegraph cable to generate current. Also shown is an eighteenth century child's thimble with holder – English enamel from south Staffordshire, looking like an exotic little duck egg; and beautiful Afghan thimbles attached to rings, which would have been part of a dowry.

Our project was a combination of motifs taken from elaborate Russian thimbles made of silver and jewel-colored enamels, making us think of ancestors leaving Russia with just enough space to pack something so beautiful.

Approximate time needed: 20 hours
Finished size of design: 8 cm (3¼ in) diameter
Yarns

Key	Anchor	Stranded Cotton	Skeins
A	387	Cream	1
B	400	Gray	2
C	1039	Turquoise	1
D	872	Mauve	1
E	341	Rust	1
F	851	Peacock	1
	Mex Ophir		**Spool**
G	301	Silver	1

Canvas

22-gauge white mono de luxe
Size: 18 x 18 cm (7¼ x 7¼ in)

Other materials

Tapestry needle, size 22
Ruler or tape measure
Masking tape for binding the canvas
Sharp scissors for cutting the canvas
Embroidery scissors
Sharp HB pencil or fine permanent marker
Eraser

Following the chart

Cut the canvas to size and bind the edges with masking tape. The design does not have to be marked out on the canvas; just follow the color chart opposite. Remember that the squares represent the canvas intersections, not the holes. Each square represents one tent stitch.

The chart is divided into units of 10 squares by 10 squares to make it easier to follow. Before stitching, it may be helpful to mark your canvas in similar units with an HB pencil or permanent marker in a suitable color. Also, we suggest

marking the top of the canvas so that, if you turn the canvas while stitching, you know where the top edge is.

The colors on the chart are shown stronger than the actual yarn colors to make them easier to see. The corresponding yarns are given in the color key.

Stitches used

TENT stitch (1), STEM stitch (2) (optional). For the stitch instructions, see page 90.

Stitching the design

Use the whole thread (three strands) of stranded cotton and two strands of silver thread. Begin in any area you wish. It might be easiest to start at the top right hand corner 4–5 cm (1½–2 in) in from the corner, working horizontally from one block of color to another. We have used STEM stitch (2) to outline the curved areas, but this is optional. If you decide to use STEM stitch in these areas, stitch the TENT stitch first.

Making up instructions

When the design has been sewn, the needlepoint may need to be stretched back into shape (see stretching instructions on page 91). Then make it up into a pincushion. The base we have used is inlaid and can be obtained from Glorafilia, or if you prefer, you can back the pincushion and stuff it with kapok or similar.

To make the design into a pincushion using our base, you will need a tapestry needle, strong thread and glue.

Thread the needle with a length of strong thread and work running stitches around the canvas about 2 cm (¾ in) outside the sewn circle to form a drawstring. Place the tapestry face down on a table and center the padded top on the tapestry with the plywood facing upwards. Pull the tapestry edges over the plywood base, pull the thread so that the edges are gathered and tie with

a bow. With a little patience ease out the gathers to attain an even finish around the edge. Glue the unsewn canvas to the plywood base. Place the padded top on the base, turn upside down and screw in.

Key

A
B
C
D
E
F
G

BLUE AND WHITE CHINA ℰ

Blue and white is the most popular, and available, china to collect: so many designs made in such quantity in so many places over so many years. For new collectors there are comprehensive books, dealers willing to share expertise, and even an enthusiasts' club.

Cobalt oxide – still used today – is a black pigment which becomes blue when fired; the technique of painting it onto white porcelain before glazing was probably pioneered in China in the fourteenth century. In the seventeenth century the Chinese began exporting huge quantities of it to Europe although, interestingly, the western world's most popular blue and white design, the Willow Pattern, did not actually come from China but was the work of Thomas Minton, on a wave of enthusiasm for things Chinese.

Around the same time, transfer printing was introduced and perfected. The patterns were transferred onto tissue from hand-engraved copper plates, and then onto white earthenware. The technique and the original plates are still in use today. Perhaps with all this blue and white, its popularity was because it looked so familiar.

We have several friends who collect blue and white china, most of them concentrating on one theme, such as a particular floral pattern or rural scenes. However, by far the most delightful collection we've seen belongs to Joan Peters, whose blue and white china fills the ground floor of her cottage. She doesn't collect by period or manufacturer, but purely on her very critical eye; the criteria being that she has to love it. Consequently, her collection is refreshingly eclectic, spanning qualities, centuries, shapes and hues. She has a remarkable homing instinct for blue and white, and we've seen her unerringly locate a beautiful ribbon plate from an unlikely pile of rubbish, and persuade a furniture dealer (correctly, as it turned out) that he must have a bit of blue and white 'somewhere at the back'.

She lives in organized serenity. The china is grouped gorgeously on every possible surface, in the knowledge that no teenager will put his Doc Martens on the mantelpiece, or a pile of unwashed laundry on the parson's table. What happens when there's no more room? Could such a passion be curbed, or does such a collector keep on collecting? The answer is yes, she keeps on collecting, will squeeze in another cabinet, will convert the bathroom to blue and white too, and finally, presumably, move house.

Joan began collecting over twenty years ago: 'I thought I'd collect a husband, but decided that china would be less trouble'. Her mother had a china shop, full of willow pattern, and couldn't understand why her daughter rejected her pristine pieces in favor of something old and possibly cracked. She remembers exactly what attracted her to the first piece she bought, which in those days could be picked up for pennies. It was a floral jug – the color had diffused into the glaze giving it the out-of-focus effect called 'flow blue' and this functional piece still sums up all she loves about blue and white: 'There is something honest about it. However decorative, blue and white is never pretentious'.

Our tiny cushion is worked on 14-gauge canvas in five shades of tapestry wool, using motifs typically found on blue and white china.

Approximate time needed: 30 hours
Finished size of design: 20 x 20 cm (8 x 8 in)
Yarns

Key	Anchor	Tapisserie Wool	Skeins
A	8000	White	6
B	8682	Pastel blue	1
C	8686	Pale blue	2
D	8644	Mid–blue	2
E	8690	Dark blue	2
F	8634	Navy	2

Canvas
14-gauge white mono de luxe
Size: 31 x 31 cm (12 x 12 in)
Other materials
Tapestry needle, size 20
Ruler or tape measure
Masking tape for binding the canvas
Sharp scissors for cutting the canvas
Embroidery scissors
Sharp HB pencil or fine permanent marker
Eraser

Following the chart
Cut the canvas to size and bind the edges with
masking tape. The design does not have to be
marked out on the canvas; just follow the color
chart opposite. Remember that the squares
represent the canvas intersections, not the holes.
Each square represents one tent stitch.

The chart is divided into units of 10 squares by
10 squares to make it easier to follow. Before
beginning to stitch, it may be helpful to mark
your canvas in similar units of 10 squares by 10
squares with an HB pencil or permanent marker
in a suitable color. Also we suggest marking the
top of the canvas so that, if you turn the canvas

while stitching, you will still know where the top
edge is.

The colors on the chart are shown stronger
than the actual yarn colors to make them easier to
see. The corresponding yarns are given in the
color key.

Stitches used
TENT stitch (1), STEM stitch (2) (optional). For
the stitch instructions, see page 90.

Stitching the design
Use the whole thread of tapisserie wool
throughout. Begin with TENT stitch (1) in any
area you wish. It might be easiest to start at the
top right hand corner 4–5 cm (1½–2 in) in from
the corner of the canvas, working horizontally
from one block of color to another. We have used
STEM stitch (2) to outline the curved areas on
the basket and the stems on the flowers but this is
optional. If you decide to use STEM stitch, this
should be done after the TENT stitch areas are
complete. Refer to the photograph of the finished
cushion for the position of STEM stitch.

Making up instructions
When the design has been sewn, the needlepoint
may need to be stretched back into shape (see
page 91). Then make it up into a cushion as
shown on page 92.

Key
A B C D E F

STAFFORDSHIRE FIGURES

Nineteenth century Staffordshire figures have a unique charm – not only are they naïve and whimsical in style, but their colors are striking and their subject matter very appealing. Their frequent lack of proportion gives them an eccentric sophistication. There are lots of eye-catching animals oozing Victorian sentimentality – and people do have a soft spot for animals, which is one of the reasons Staffordshire has become such a prized collectable. Imagine an archetypal aunt's mantlepiece, carriage clock centre, bracketed by candlesticks, photographs, miscellanea . . . wouldn't there always be Staffordshire pieces at each end with rather disdainful expressions?

The figures are often historically interesting, depicting villains as well as heroes, all in the same simple jolly style. Gerald Clark, whose menagerie we photographed, remembers the first piece of Staffordshire he ever bought. It was the highwayman Dick Turpin on horseback, and it was the simplicity of the piece that drew him to it. He collected for ten years before he started dealing in Staffordshire, and acknowledges the sad Catch-22 situation of being unable to be both collector and dealer – there is the temptation to keep too many pieces.

Staffordshire pottery began as cottage art, it was pottery made for the people and sold at street corners by pedlars. Cheap child labor was used in the factories which explains why painted decoration may be incomplete or irregular, an 'N' the wrong way round, or letters in reversed order. Employees were employed for their capable hands, not for their literacy.

Staffordshire is now a generic name, also referring to pottery made in northern England, in Newcastle and around Castleford, Yorkshire, and in Portobello, close to Edinburgh. As with most things, there is no easy way to learn about Staffordshire – just by looking and looking, and handling as much as you can, feeling the difference in weight and finish. Genuine pieces are often surprisingly light. Some particularly complex pieces were made in separate molds and joined together. Molds were found when the factories closed down and these are still being used by people turning out reproductions – the objects are similar, the difference is in the colors. Fakers and restorers may be very skilled, but the colors of the original highly toxic leaded paints cannot be successfully imitated.

We have tried to give our needlepoint dogs the same expression as their counterparts: world-weary rather than bored, and just this side of irritated. They have a look that suggests another ten minutes standing here is the limit of endurance, so could the photographer please get a move on. Over the years we have produced many differently shaped animals, a whole zoo-full, and yet these are the first Staffordshire creatures, and perhaps the most successful. Their immobility looks just right. It would be possible to make a whole set, in different sizes, by using the same chart scaled up and down on different gauges of canvas. Tapestry wool could be used on 14, 12 and 10 canvas, while 18 canvas could be stitched in cotton and 7 canvas could use tapestry wool double. Anything bigger, 3 canvas for example, would look more like a Great Dane rather than a spaniel.

Approximate time needed: 17 hours for each dog
Finished size of design: 16 x 21 cm (6¼ x 8¼ in)

Yarns

Key	Anchor	Tapisserie Wool	Skeins
A	8000	White	4
B	9422	Apricot	2
C	9526	Copper	2
D	9562	Terracotta	4
E	9542	Dark terracotta	3
F	9566	Chocolate	2
G	9774	Gray	2
H	9362	Cream	2
I	9366	Beige	2
	Anchor Stranded Cotton		
J	403	Black	1

These yarn quantities make two dogs. Reverse the chart for the second dog.

Canvas

14-gauge white mono de luxe
Size: 26 x 31 cm (10¼ x 12¼ in) for each dog

Other materials

Tapestry needle, size 20
Ruler or tape measure
Masking tape for binding the canvas
Sharp scissors for cutting the canvas
Embroidery scissors
Sharp HB pencil or fine permanent marker
Eraser

Following the chart

Cut canvas to size and bind edges with tape. The design does not have to be marked out on the canvas; just follow chart opposite. The squares represent the canvas intersections, not the holes. Each square represents one tent stitch.

The chart is divided into units of 10 squares by 10 squares to make it easier to follow. Before stitching, it may be helpful to mark your canvas in similar units with a pencil or permanent marker. Mark the top of the canvas so that if you turn the canvas while stitching you known where the top is.

Stitches used

TENT stitch (1), STEM stitch (2) (optional). For stitch instructions, see page 90.

Stitching the design

Use the whole thread of tapisserie wool and the whole thread (six strands) of stranded cotton. Begin with TENT stitch (1) in any area you wish. It might be easiest to start at the top right hand corner 4–5 cm (1½–2 in) in from the corner of the canvas, working horizontally from one block of color to another.

STEM stitch (2) in black stranded cotton outlines the eyes, eyebrows, nose, mouth and neck. STEM stitch should be done after the TENT stitch areas are complete. Refer to the photo for the position of STEM stitch.

Making up instructions

When the design has been sewn, the needlepoint may need to be stretched back into shape (see page 91). To make it up into a cushion you will need 25 cm (10 in) felt, pins and terylene/kapok.

After you have stretched the dog back into shape, make a paper pattern by tracing around the edge of the dog. Cut out the felt, adding 1 cm (½ in) all around for seams. The design should also be cut out leaving a 1 cm (½ in) border of unsewn canvas. With right sides together, tack the felt to the tapestry sewing close to the design. Then machine or back stitch, leaving an opening of 7.5 cm (3 in). Turn back to the right side and stuff. Using slip stitch, close the opening.

Key

A
B
C
D
E
F
G
H
I
J

MAJOLICA

When we had our first Glorafilia shop in the 1960s, we were offered a Minton majolica piece. It was very tall, a jardinière supported by herons and foliage, outrageously, theatrically decorative. Oh no, we said, isn't it a bit, well, excessive? Majolica is an acquired taste, and unfortunately we had not yet acquired it. Not many other people in Britain have acquired it either, judging by the fact that the majority of majolica goes to America. Americans understand the humor and the imagination behind majolica, and are not afraid to put the flamboyant ochers, cobalt and turquoise, sugar pinks and marvellous greens in their homes. British collectors and dealers know that in a few years the British are going to wake up to what they have let slip away!

The name is a confusing one. Maiolica is Italian for tin-glazed earthenware, the name derived from Majorca, the island that imported it into Renaissance Italy from North Africa and the East. Majolica, on the other hand, is a Victorian form of opaque colored glaze, whose nearest relative is the multi-colored earthenware made in fifteenth century Florence. Or, to put it another way, Londoners call swedes turnips and the Scots call turnips swedes.

Majolica pieces usually announce what they're for. Asparagus dishes flaunt relief-molded asparagus. A game dish may have a dead partridge atop, cheese dishes a cow. There are ninety different styles of strawberry dish (many Victorians had hothouses), crocus pots, salt containers, fish platters spread with huge fish, sardine boxes for sardines that came dried in small wooden containers, teapots in the shape of monkeys – one of the most enduring majolica images. There are also pieces formed from perhaps twenty sections – huge extravagancies of linked cherubs, lush vegetation, rams' heads, cornucopia – created for London's Great Exhibition of 1862, as well as whole facades of tiles combining renaissance, neo-classical and rococo influences.

Currently the most desirable piece of majolica, we are told, is a game dish. It looks very Alice in Wonderland: two rabbits and a whimsical mallard. It is desirable because collectors often specialize and there are too many collectors chasing too few pieces. We heard of one collector closing in on a long sought-after piece, check book in outstretched hand, to be beaten by a fax sliding through the machine as he approached the counter. There is the story of a couple making an annual pilgrimage across the Atlantic to track down a particular piece, only to find it in the eighteenth year with a 'sold' sticker on it, and the new purchaser refusing to sell. In such a case, the hysteria of disappointment and pain does little good. Nor does the adage 'everyone has a price'.

English majolica peaked in the second half of the nineteenth century, making a huge global impact. The palette of vibrant colors was achieved through laborious experimentation, testing recipes until the lustrous glazes were perfected. Later, when it was realized that the lead in the glazes was highly toxic the factories closed, and the imitations that followed could not match the same depth of brilliance.

We have used motifs and colors from a multitude of different majolica pieces to create our little fringed cushion.

Approximate time needed: 30 hours
Finished size of design: 21 x 18 cm (8 x 7 in)
Yarns

Key	Anchor	Tapisserie Wool	Skeins
A	8000	White	1
B	8056	Pale yellow	2
C	8058	Gold	2
D	9018	Apple green	2
E	9006	Grass green	2
F	8806	Turquoise	1
G	8366	Pink	1
H	8368	Rose pink	1
I	8584	Lilac	1
J	8604	Violet	1
K	9600	Ginger	2
L	8692	Royal blue	3

Canvas
14-gauge white mono de luxe
Size: 31 x 28 cm (12 x 11 in)

Other materials
Tapestry needle, size 20
Ruler or tape measure
Masking tape for binding the canvas
Sharp scissors for cutting the canvas
Embroidery scissors
Sharp HB pencil or fine permanent marker
Eraser

Following the chart
Cut canvas to size and bind edges with masking tape. The design does not have to be marked out on the canvas; just follow the color chart opposite. The squares represent the canvas intersections, not the holes. Each square represents one tent stitch.

The chart is divided into units of 10 squares by 10 squares to make it easier to follow. Before stitching, it may be helpful to mark your canvas in similar units with a pencil or permanent marker in a suitable color. Mark the top of the canvas so that if you turn the canvas while stitching you know where the top is.

The colors on the chart are shown stronger than the actual yarn colors to make them easier to see. The corresponding yarns are given in the color key.

Stitches used
TENT stitch (1), STEM stitch (2) (optional). For stitch instructions, see page 90.

Stitching the design
Use the whole thread of tapisserie wool throughout. Begin in any area you wish. It might be easiest to start at the top right hand corner 4–5 cm (1½–2 in) in from the corner of the canvas, working horizontally from one block of color to another. We have used STEM stitch (2) on the green stems of the flowers and leaves. If you decide to use STEM stitch, this should be done after the TENT stitch. Refer to the photograph of the finished cushion for the position of STEM stitch.

Making up instructions
When the design has been sewn, the needlepoint may need to be stretched back into shape (see page 91). Make into a cushion as on page 92.

Key
A B C D E F G H I J K L

SAMPLERS ℭ

Samplers are a social curiosity, and it is the workmanship rather than the aesthetic beauty that is fascinating – look at enough samplers and the eye becomes used to the staccato effect of the naïve elements. Sampler, essemplair, something to be an example, a necessary record of stitches and patterns to be copied and passed to a daughter, and she in turn to her daughter, to preserve mending and decorative skills now mostly forgotten.

They were also worked by children and both American and English samplers include pious moral tracts. These were sometimes inscribed 'wrought by ' (wrought to rhyme with fraught) and wrought they were – not only in silks and wools, but hair and fabric and braid, pearls and beads. 'This work in hands my friends may have, when I am dead and laid in grave' by Sarah Warner aged nine. Poor Sarah, with her determined landscape and grisly verse . . . Margaret Mutter, also nine, who wrought a laughing reindeer apparently on roller-skates . . . Phoebe Moulton, aged ten, and her skillful Edgar Allen Poe sheep, and poor Clarissa Kimball with a ditty about death standing at the door. Mary Dudden embroidered that she 'were twelve years of age when this sampler were worked, and some part of it by moonlight'. The younger the child, the more desirably collectable the sampler. Perhaps we should have present-day equivalents to the verses: 'When I am dead and in my grave, think of all the tax I'll save'. Or 'The grounds he cited for divorce: excessive use of pesto sauce'.

With the advent of pattern books, samplers became less individual and more an increasingly stereotyped schoolgirl discipline. In the ephemera of the twentieth century, what is the equivalent of the sampler? Surely not the sensible blouses we were all compelled to make at school? In the eighteenth century it was not unique for a whole Bible chapter to be embroidered – today some of us are awestruck if offspring manage to chain stitch their initials onto a gym-bag. Is skill now restricted to the speed with which a Nintendo game can be despatched?

What chance would we have today to encourage our free thinking, instant-gratification children to make something as ambitious as a sampler? In our shop, all except the simplest kits are thought too complex for small children: too discouraging, too time consuming, too fine, too subtle . . . what about Sarah Warner, we want to say, Clarissa Kimball? But then, at nine, they were preparing for their own mortality, so things have changed a bit.

The first sampler we bought at auction sent us into such a frenzy that we had our knuckles rapped for bidding against ourselves. It was unusually colorful, with bold extravagant baskets and figures, and some shrunken squirrels (one of whom had apparently chewed through part of the background). We still have it and would be very loathe to part with it.

Our sampler project takes elements from traditional samplers of the eighteenth and nineteenth centuries, with typical muted colors and lack of perspective. It can easily be personalized as we have shown, or other horizontal bands inserted to add more details: a few pages of *Finnegan's Wake*, some psalms, a sonnet, the complete works of Shakespeare, what you will.

Approximate time needed: 40 hours

Finished size of design: 16 x 21 cm (6¼ x 8¼ in)

Yarns

Key	Anchor	Stranded Cotton	Skeins
A	852	Cream	7
B	888	Ocher	2
C	859	Pale green	1
D	262	Mid-green	1
E	879	Bottle green	1
F	371	Chestnut	2
G	883	Orange	1
H	893	Pink	1
I	1018	Purple	1
J	921	Blue	1

Canvas

18-gauge white mono deluxe
Size: 26 x 31 cm (10¼ x 12¼ in)

Other materials

Tapestry needle, size 22
Ruler or tape measure
Masking tape for binding the canvas
Sharp scissors for cutting the canvas
Embroidery scissors
Sharp HB pencil or fine permanent marker
Eraser

Following the chart

Cut the canvas to size and bind the edges with masking tape. The design does not have to be marked out on the canvas; just follow the color chart opposite. Remember that the squares represent the canvas intersections, not the holes. Each square represents one tent stitch.

The chart is divided into units of 10 squares by 10 squares to make it easier to follow. Before stitching, it may be helpful to mark your canvas in similar units with a pencil or permanent marker in a suitable color. Mark the top of the canvas so that if you turn the canvas while stitching you know where the top is.

The colors on the chart are shown stronger than the actual yarn colors to make them easier to see. The corresponding yarns are given in the color key.

Stitches used

TENT stitch (1), STEM stitch (2) (optional). For the stitch instructions, see page 90.

Stitching the design

Use the whole thread (six strands) of stranded cotton throughout. Begin in any area you wish. It might be easiest to start at the top right hand corner of the canvas, 4–5 cm (1½–2 in) in from the corner, working horizontally from one block of color to another. Before you stitch the background of area **A**, decide the date you want using the number/letter chart on page 88. Plan it on graph paper. You may have to shorten the date or use numbers only. Stitch the date in TENT stitch (1) followed by the background. When you reach area **B**, outline the circle using STEM stitch (2) and then trace the initials you require from the initial sheet overleaf, using a pencil or permanent marker. Stitch the initials in STEM stitch (2) followed by the background in TENT stitch (1).

Making up instructions

Many needlepointers feel experienced enough to stretch and make up their needlepoint picture designs, but we feel that a needlepoint should be framed by a professional experienced in stretching and framing needlepoint.

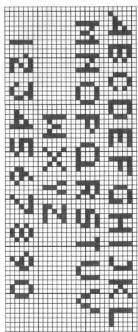

Chart for area **Ⓐ**

Chart for area **Ⓑ** – see next page

Key

A
B
C
D
E
F
G
H
I
J

Chart for area Ⓑ

GENERAL INFORMATION ℰ

MARKING THE CANVAS

Always leave a border of at least 5 cm (2 in) of unstitched canvas all around the edges of the design for stretching purposes.

When marking a canvas into squares of 10 threads by 10 threads, use a permanent marker in a suitable color, an HB pencil or a water-erasable marking pen.

STITCHING

The colors shown on the charts are stronger than the actual yarn colors to make them easier to see. The corresponding yarns are given in the color keys.

When working from a chart, start at the top right hand corner 5 cm (2 in) in from the edge. Stitch horizontally from one block of color to another.

We suggest you use the basketweave method on a large area of tent stitch (see page 90) as it does not put a strain on the canvas and a more even tension is achieved.

White yarn should be left until last to keep it clean. Don't let the ends of other colors get caught into the stitches.

WORKING METHODS

We normally suggest that you use a frame when stitching, but this is a personal choice. However, the needlepoint projects in this book are all quite small and a frame is not essential. Just try not to pull the yarn too tightly.

Some people need a thimble, and at some point in your needlepoint career you may well need a seam unpicker!

YARN

We have used Anchor Tapisserie yarn, stranded cotton or metallic thread in all our projects.

Anchor tapisserie wool is 100% pure new wool, color-fast and of a tightly twisted construction. It comes in 475 color-matched and co-ordinated shades in 10 meter (11 yard) skeins.

Anchor stranded cotton is a superior 6-strand, mercerised cotton embroidery thread in 8 meter (8½ yard) skeins, available in 444 color-balanced and co-ordinated shades. It is divisible into separate strands.

Mez Astrella gold thread is 50% polyester, 50% metal. ***Mez Ophir*** silver thread is 60% viscose, 40% polyester metal.

Cut your tapestry wool into lengths of 75 cm (30 in); cut stranded cotton and silver/gold thread into 38–50 cm (15–20 in) lengths.

To begin, knot the wool temporarily on the front of the canvas about 2.5 cm (1 in) from where you want to start, in the direction in which you will be working. As you work your canvas, the stitches on the back will anchor the 2.5cm (1 in) thread. When you reach the knot, cut it off and the thread should be quite secure. When you re-thread your needle to continue sewing the same area, there is no need to knot the wool; simply run the needle through the work on the underside. To finish, do the same in reverse.

Keep the back of the canvas tidy for two simple reasons. Firstly, having lots of ends hanging at the back can eventually make it difficult to get your needle through the canvas. Secondly, the work will lie flatter when it is made up. So cut your threads short when you have anchored them.

Continental Tent Stitch

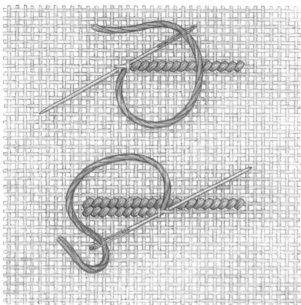

Basketweave Stitch

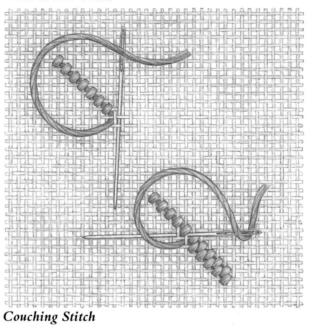

Stem Stitch

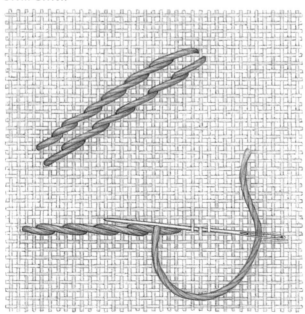

Couching Stitch

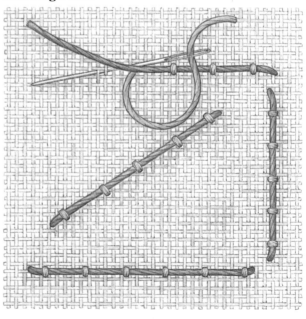

STITCHES
1 TENT STITCH

TENT stitch, which forms a fine background of short slanting stitches, can be worked in a number of different ways.

CONTINENTAL TENT stitch is worked *horizontally* across the canvas from right to left. At the end of the row, turn the canvas upside down and work the next row, again from right to left.

VERTICAL TENT stitch should only be used for single *vertical* lines, e.g. outlining.

BASKETWEAVE TENT stitch is worked *diagonally* from the top right hand corner without turning the canvas. This is the best stitch to use on larger areas of background as it does not distort the canvas.

2 STEM STITCH

STEM stitch is useful for flower stems or outlining faces or other features, as in the doll or the tennis picture. Work from left to right following the diagram on the left, making sure the stitches are of a similar length. Each stitch slightly overlaps the previous one.

3 COUCHING

This stitch is used in the perfume sachet and the jewelry roll. The simplest and most straightforward method of couching is shown in the diagram on the left. One long thread is couched down by several single small threads at equal intervals. Hold the single thread in place with the left thumb and couch down with a tiny stitch. Do not allow the long thread to pucker. The couching down stitch should be firm. This stitch can be worked horizontally, vertically or diagonally, as shown in the diagram.

CARING FOR FINISHED PIECES

Just as we would never cover an oil painting with glass, we never use glass on a framed needlepoint. To keep needlepoint pictures clean, just flick over with a feather duster. Needlepoint can be Scotch-Guarded and we strongly recommend that you do not wash it. Take it to a dry cleaner instead.

FINISHING AND MAKING UP

Many needlepointers feel experienced enough to stretch and make up their needlework designs into cushions, bags, pincushions and other items, but we always feel that a needlepoint picture or photograph frame should be dealt with by an experienced professional. Consequently, we do not give instructions for the framed pictures and photograph frame.

The finishing instructions for the other needlepoint projects in this book appear on the page where the stitching instructions are. The exceptions are the cushions, perfume sachet, lace pincushion, jewelry roll, spectacles case and bookmark which are on pages 91–92.

Stretching

If you wish to stretch your needlepoint before making up, use the following method.

The needlepoint must be 'square' before framing or making into a cushion, bag, pincushion, etc. If it is out of square, lightly dampen or spray it and leave for a few minutes to soften the canvas. Gently pull square and then pin out, right side down, on to blotting paper on a clean, flat board. Use tacks, staples or drawing pins and pin outside the sewn surface. Do not strain the canvas too tightly or the needlepoint will dry with a scalloped edge.

When the needlepoint is thoroughly dry (this may take two or three days), remove it from the board.

FRILLED PINCUSHION/CUSHION/ SACHET

Fabric – you will need 50 cm (20 in) of fabric if
   you are making a frill from the backing fabric.
   If you use braid or lace, you will need less
   fabric. You will require fabric 5 cm (2 in)
   bigger than the sewn area for the backing.
If you use braid or lace you will need two and a
   half times around the sewn edges.
If you pipe the pincushion/cushion, you will
   need piping cord and enough fabric to cover
   the piping cord. Alternatively, you can use plain
   cord.
pins
kapok or terylene filling
pot pourri (for the perfume sachet)

1 Stretch the needlepoint back to the original
shape (see page 90).
2 Gather the fabric frill or the lace frill by hand or
machine.
3 Cut away excess canvas leaving 1 cm (½ in) of
unsewn canvas for turning.
4 If you decide to pipe the pincushion/cushion,
do it now using piping cord covered with fabric.
5 Tack the gathered frill to the right side of the
needlepoint, pushing more gathers into each
corner. Join the ends of the frill together and
machine into place.
6 Tack or pin the back panel onto the
needlepoint, right sides together. Machine the
back panel close to the edge of the needlepoint
leaving a 8 cm (3 in) opening.
7 If you decide to use cord, sew it on before you
stuff. For a perfume sachet, mix the stuffing with
pot pourri. Slip stitch the opening.

CUSHION WITH NEEDLEPOINT PANEL

25 cm (10 in) fabric
pins
50 cm (20 in) fringing
1 meter (1 yard) braid
kapok or terylene filling

1 Stretch the needlepoint back into its original
shape (see page 90) and cut away any excess
canvas, leaving 1.5 cm (½ in) of unsewn canvas
for turning.
2 Cut two pieces of fabric for the side panels 5 cm
(2 in) wide by the depth of the needlepoint, plus
turnings.
3 Cut out the fabric for the cushion backing to
measure as follows: the same depth as the side
panels (including turnings) plus the two panel
widths plus the width of the needlepoint in the
center (plus turnings).
4 Tack or pin the front panels into place next to
the needlepoint and machine close to the finished
needlepoint. Sew the fringe neatly along the seam
line.
5 Tack cushion back to cushion front, right sides
together. Machine around the edge, leaving
15 cm (6 in) opening at the bottom. Turn the
cushion to the right side.
6 Sew the braid around the edge of the cushion,
starting from a corner. Join the two ends neatly.
Stuff with kapok or terylene filling, and slip stitch
the opening together.

JEWELRY ROLL

25 cm (10 in) fabric
1 meter (1 yard) piping cord
pins
press stud
60 cm (24 in) ribbon

1 Stretch the needlepoint back to the original shape (see page 90).
2 Cut away the excess canvas, leaving 1.5 cm (½ in) of unsewn canvas for turning. Cut out a piece of fabric 33 x 23 cm (13 x 9 in) for the lining, two pieces 18 x 23 cm (7 x 9 in) for the pockets, and two strips 6 x 23 cm (2½ x 9 in) for the two center strips for holding rings, bracelets, earrings, etc.
3 If you decide to pipe the jewelry roll, this is the time to do it. Cut the piping strips on the cross and pipe around the needlepoint.
4 Fold the pocket pieces in half and tack or pin to each end of the lining, right sides together. Fold the strips in half, taking 1.5 cm (½ in) turning. Machine together and turn through to the right side and press. Tack to the right side of the lining 3 cm (1¼ in) from the top of the pockets and machine into place.
5 Stitch both ends of one of the strips to the side of the jewelry roll, and stitch one end of the other strip to the jewelry roll. The other end can be secured by a press stud (to enable the strip to be undone for rings and bracelets).
6 With right sides together, tack into place and machine around, leaving a 10 cm (4 in) opening. Trim turnings away from the corners, and turn to the right side. Slip stitch the opening together.
7 Sew on the ribbon to secure the jewelry roll.

SPECTACLE CASE

25 cm (10 in) fabric
pins
1 Trim canvas leaving 1 cm (½ in) border of unsewn canvas. Cut out backing and another two pieces the same size as the canvas.
2 With right sides of the case and backing facing, stitch as close to the design as possible, leaving top open.
3 Turn back to the right side and hem down the top of the canvas and the backing.
4 Machine the lining right sides together taking a 1 cm (½ in) turning. Put the lining inside the spectacle case, turn down the top of the lining and hem to the top of the spectacle case.

BOOKMARK

piece of fabric 26 x 8 cm (10 x 3 in)
pins
1 Trim canvas leaving a 1 cm (½ in) border of unsewn canvas. Cut out backing the same size as the canvas.
2 Right sides facing, tack together leaving the top open. Stitch close to the finished work.
3 Cut straight across the corners, leaving 5 mm (¼ in) so that it will lay flat. Turn back to the right side and neaten the top.
4 For the tassel, cut 12 strands of cotton 76 cm (30 in) long. Fold in half and half again.
5 Take a strand of yarn and wrap round the center. With the excess strand of yarn make a loop. Make three crochet chains from the loop.
6 Fold at the chain and with another strand of yarn wrap around 1 cm (½ in) from the top. Finish off. Cut the loops at the bottom and sew onto bookmark.

YARN SUPPLIERS

For details of stockists and mail order sources of the yarns used in this book, please contact the following addresses:

Coats Patons Crafts
PO Box McMullen Road
Darlington
Co Durham
DL1 1YQ
UK

Coats Patons Crafts
89–91 Peters Avenue
Mulgrave
Victoria 3170
Australia

Coats Canada Inc
1001 Roselawn Avenue
Toronto
Ontario
M6B 1B8
Canada

Coats & Clark Inc
PO Box 24998
Greenville
SC 29616-2498
USA

Coats Patons (New Zealand)
PO Box 51–645
263 Ti Rakau Drive
Pakuranga
Auckland
New Zealand

MATERIALS AND KITS SERVICE

Glorafilia can provide all the materials needed to complete each project in this book: canvas cut to size and taped at the edges, the correct needles and enough yarn to complete the design, and various items of equipment that you may need.

Complete kits

Some of the designs are available as complete kits. If you would like to receive information on which designs are available, or to order materials directly, write to Glorafilia.

Glorafilia Ltd
The Old Mill House
The Ridgeway
Mill Hill Village
London NW7 4EB
Tel: 081 906 0212, fax: 081 959 6253

Marsha Kear
510 Weadley Road
King of Prussia PA 19406
USA
Tel/fax: 610 688 4864

ACKNOWLEDGMENTS

Our thanks to Coats Patons Crafts for supplying us with the yarn and for all their help with this project. And to our team of superb stitchers: Mary Clark, Andrea Cooper, Josephine Farhoumand, Evelyn Genis, Vicki Henley, Joyce Talbot and Barbara Williams.

A special thanks to those whose collections feature in this book. They are:

Sheila Crown (the frog collection)
Sally King (tennis memorabilia)
Joan Peters (blue and white china)
Doreen Turner (lace bobbins)

Rita Smythe (majolica)
Britannia
Grays Antique Market
58 Davies Street
London W1
Tel: 071 629 6772

Marlborough Rare Books Ltd (antiquarian books)
144–146 New Bond Street
London W1Y 9FD
Tel: 071 493 6993, fax: 071 499 2479

Bridget McConnel (thimbles)
The Thimble Society of London
Grays Antique Market
58 Davies Street
London W1
Tel: 071 493 0560

Lynn Holmes (agate jewelry)
Stand 305–6, Gray's Antique Market
58 Davies Street
London W1
Tel: 071 629 7327

Gerald Clark Antiques (Staffordshire figures)
1 High Street
Mill Hill Village
London NW7
Tel: 081 958 4249

Anne Fortescue (bags and purses)
Portwine Arcade
175 Portobello Road
London W11
Tel: 071 381 5674

David and Gisela Barrington (antique dolls)
Angel Arcade
118 Islington High Street
London N1 8EG
Tel: 071 354 1601 (Weds and Sats)

Noel Gibson (tartanware)
Eureka Antiques
105 Portobello Road
London W11
Tel: 061 941 5453

Pam Hebbs (teddy bears)
5 The Annexe
Camden Passage
London N1
Tel: 081 361 3739 (evenings)

Edward Bramah (teapots)
Bramah Tea and Coffee Museum
The Clove Building
Maguire Street
Butlers Wharf
London SE1 2NQ
Tel: 071 378 0222, fax: 071 378 0219

Teresa Clayton (perfume bottles)
Trio, Stand L24
Grays Mews Antique Market
1–7 Davies Mews
London W1
Tel: 071 629 1184

Lesley Bell-Gibson (samplers)
Red Lion Arcade, Stall 15
165–169 Portobello Road
London W11 (Sats 9.30am – 4.00pm)